How Organizations Work

Taking a Holistic Approach to Enterprise Health

ALAN P. BRACHE

JOHN WILEY & SONS, INC.

Copyright © 2002 by Kepner-Tregoe, Inc. All rights reserved.

Published by John Wiley & Sons, Inc., New York.

Published simultaneously in Canada.

This publication is designed to provide accurate and authoritative information in regard to the subject manner covered. It is sold with the understanding that the publisher is not engaged in rendering legal, accounting, or other professional services. If legal advice or other expert assistance is required, the services of a competent professional person should be sought.

Library of Congress Cataloging-in-Publication Data:

Brache, Alan P., 1950–
    How organizations work : taking a holistic approach to enterprise health /
Alan P. Brache.
        p.   cm.
    Includes bibliographical references and index.
    ISBN 0-471-20033-6 (cloth : alk. paper)
        1. Organizational effectiveness. 2. Organizational change.
3. Management. I. Title.
    HD58.9. .B73 2001
    658.4'06—dc21   2001045309

Contents

Foreword

Whether you run, or work for, a manufacturer, a distributor, a financial institution, a government agency, a dotcom or telecom, or an organization of just about any size and type, chances are you and your colleagues face the relentless challenge of improving performance.

There are, of course, many paths to raising performance and achieving greater levels of business results. Regardless of which path they've followed, those who have made the trek are often disappointed. Their hard-won changes—whether in customer service, quality, cycle time, cost containment, morale, or safety—tend to be short lived. The reason: They haven't zeroed in on the root cause of the issues or the factors necessary for successful, permanent resolution.

Here's the fundamental flaw that Alan Brache points to in his powerful new book: Executives and managers just don't know how to pull the right levers, in the right way, at the right time. As a result, major problems recur; opportunities slip away; changes don't last; and the resources invested in improvement efforts yield little, if any, return. The costs can be enormous in terms of an organization's financial health, its competitive position, and its employee morale.

Alan's book offers a clear and integrated solution to remedy this flaw. He presents a new "Enterprise Model," one that takes into account all the variables that influence performance. What you get from *How Organizations Work* is a 360-degree picture of organizational dynamics and how they may be harnessed to effect permanent improvements in performance.

The book establishes an interactive relationship with the reader by raising a set of questions with which to check his or her organization's vital signs. After conducting this comprehensive physical exam, the reader comes away from the book with a complete understanding of the state of the organization's health.

While bookstores are littered with volumes on change management and performance improvement, Alan's book stands apart: It is based on a comprehensive model; it focuses on the basics of blocking and tackling rather than on airy theorizing about change; it is a quick and easy read; its diagnostic orientation encourages reader involvement. *How Organizations Work* sets out to break the source code of performance improvement.

The book is aimed at executives and managers at every level, especially those new to their job, those whose performance-improvement efforts have not produced the expected results— a vast audience indeed—those facing major change issues, and those with strengths in a limited number of areas who need to reach beyond them to make their change efforts succeed.

Alan's book is concise and written for executives and managers who are searching for practical concepts and approaches to help their organization become more effective and better places to be. *How Organizations Work* should prove to be the discovery for which they have been waiting.

Rich Teerlink
Retired Chairman/CEO
Harley-Davidson, Inc.

Acknowledgments

My thanks to:

Violet and Paul Brache, my parents, for encouraging me to pursue a career that they find difficult to understand.

Ben Tregoe, cofounder of Kepner-Tregoe, for introducing me to workplace learning, the contributions that can be made by a consultant, and the power of rational thinking.

The late Tom Gilbert, cofounder of the Praxis Corporation, for helping me understand the factors that influence human performance.

Geary Rummler, my former partner in the Rummler-Brache Group, for awakening me to the central role of business processes.

My clients at Kepner-Tregoe and at the Rummler-Brache Group, who provided the crucibles in which the ideas in this book were formed.

Peter Tobia, my literary agent, for honing my message, managing our side of the publication process, and enabling me to be one of those fortunate authors who doesn't need to get his hands dirty with financial matters.

Bill Butterfield, my document coordinator, for his infectious serenity, can-do responses to my requests, and patience with the numerous revisions of the manuscript of this book.

And, finally, special thanks to Larry Alexander and Matt Holt of John Wiley for their encouragement, support, and guidance.

Exploring the New Enterprise Model

■ AVOIDING THE CHANGE TRAP

A couple of years ago, I addressed an in-house group of telecommunications company executives. I was introduced by the quality director, who was concerned that my message would be seen as too complex for the "distill it to three bullet points" orientation of this group. She wisely began by saying, "We talk a lot about making things simple, and that is good; however, we do not want to make things simpler than they are."

If organizations were simple, we would have broken the code long ago. The typical company or agency would be a well-oiled machine. However, even small enterprises are typically a complex network of interlocking factors.

Executives, most often characterized by short attention spans, dissatisfaction with the status quo, and impatience with the mere mortals in their employ, delight in launching crusades. As in the Middle Ages, the objectives of these improvement crusades are to capture the Holy Land (the target market) and to convert the infidels (prospective customers and current/potential employees) to the faith. Like the Christian Crusades, they are launched with religious fervor. They are well funded. They are highly visible. They are championed by true believers. They are populated with the best and brightest. And they produce mixed results.

Sometimes these improvement crusades are massive and multiyear. In the late 1980s, we saw quality crusades. In the early 1990s, reengineering was the cause célèbre. In the late 1990s, the business landscape was awash in enterprise resource planning. The early 2000s have been characterized by acquisitions juggernauts, modeled after the growth strategy of companies like GE and Tyco. Along the way, these holy wars have spawned denominations and cults that pursue subcrusades that ride under banners such as Six Sigma, high-performance teams, supply chain management, cycle time reduction, activity-based costing, and the balanced scorecard.

The noble intent of these initiatives is beyond question, as is the sincerity of the beliefs that underpin them. The issue is the degree to which growth and efficiency programs (1) address an organization's unique needs, (2) cover all of the variables that influence their success, and (3) are sustained long enough to achieve their objectives.

To change metaphors, improving organizational health is like improving human health. If there were a pill, exercise program, or diet regimen that cured all ills and prevented future maladies, doctors would have even more time for golf. The elixirs that claim to address the full spectrum of physical wellness make it "simpler than it is." The same is true of the potions that tout organizational wellness.

■ GETTING TO ORGANIZATIONAL HEALTH

Even after a few thousand years of study, the functionality of a human being—especially the nonmechanical aspects of behavior and performance—is not fully understood. While the owner's manual will become more complete as insights are derived from the recently sequenced genome, mysteries will remain. However, three truths have emerged from the study of anatomy, physiology, and psychology:

1. Each organ, muscle, bone, and nerve plays a unique role.

2. An outstanding contribution from one component of the body-mind engine (well-developed muscles, a robust heart, a strong sense of smell, a quick wit) can not fully compensate for deficiencies in another com-

ponent (low-capacity lungs, a broken wrist, impaired hearing, poor short-term memory).

3. The understanding of each component does not provide a complete explanation of a person's health. Like a sports team, which may be less or more effective than the sum of its individual players' talents, a body is an integrated system in which the interactions are as important as the individual roles.

These same truths hold true for an organization, be it a business, a part of a business (profit center, product line, region, department, plant, store), a government agency, a union, a charity, a church, or even a family. Organizational health is a function of understanding and managing an intricate and entwined set of variables.

■ CHANGING ORGANIZATIONAL DNA

Most people, including those without any visible signs of disease, do not optimize their physical and mental fitness or establish the foundation of a long, healthy life. Similarly, most organizations do not follow a diet and exercise program that maximizes performance. Why? Because most executives and managers:

- *Do not understand the factors that influence health.* They are probably aware of the importance of leadership and goals and structure, for example, but may not fully grasp the nature and extent of the impact that each has on performance.
- *Do not understand how the factors interact.* For example, they may not appreciate the ways in which culture affects decision making or the nuances of the symbiotic relationship between business processes and skills.
- *Do not know the actions they need to take to manage their organization's health.* For example, they may know that information systems need to serve the strategy but not understand how to make that happen. They may understand conceptually that reward systems need to be linked to business processes but not know how to align them.

- *Focus on one or two variables, rather than the whole system.* They embark on a culture transformation effort or an enterprise resource planning (ERP) system installation or a Total Productive Maintenance initiative without considering the effect of and on other variables. Like other integrated systems—the human body, an automobile engine, a multilateral trade alliance—tinkering with one component can have a positive or negative effect on other components.

Is there anything that is hardwired? The answer is no. Organizations have DNA, made up of their historical products/services, markets, brand, and culture. However, unlike in the human body, organizational DNA can be changed. The transformation begins with understanding.

■ PRESCRIPTION FOR ORGANIZATIONAL WELLNESS

A program for managing your organization's health is founded on the answers to four questions:

1. What are the variables that influence your organization's performance?
2. What is the role that each variable should perform?
3. How do the variables interact in a way that contributes to your overall performance mosaic?
4. What can you do to improve performance?

Organizational wellness, like human wellness, is a destination that is never reached. The remainder of this book uses these four questions as the vehicles for describing the journey. To begin, we need an organization model that is the rough equivalent of a cutaway view of the human body. This Enterprise Model,[1] Figure 1.1, will serve as the anchor for our exploration of performance improvement.

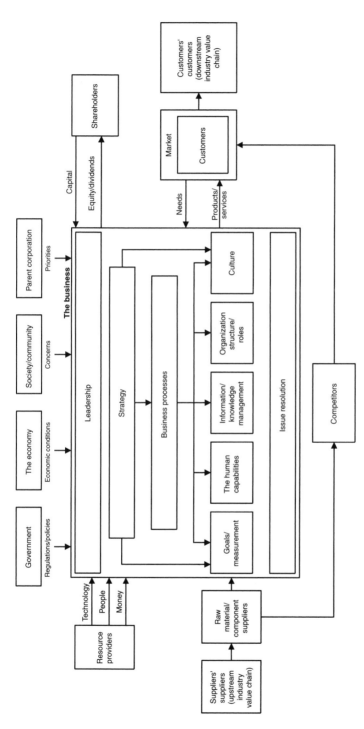

Figure 1.1 The Enterprise Model

■ ORGANIZATION PERFORMANCE: KNOWING THE VARIABLES

At the most macro level, there are two sets of performance variables: those that are outside the organization (and, in many cases, outside its control) and those that are internal (and often seem to be out of control). There are three factors in the internal equation: structural variables, human variables, and variables that have both a structural and human dimension.

What Are the External Variables?

Effective physicians and psychologists understand that long-term wellness programs are based on an understanding not only of patients' inner workings but also of external influences on them. Similarly, you are better able to improve your organization's performance if you understand its context, which is made up of these components:

- *Customers and customers' customers.* The price of admission to the world-class performance game is "profound knowledge" of your customers and the not-yet-customers in your target markets. If your customers are not end users, you can better meet their needs if you know the requirements and buying criteria of those whom they serve.

  An industry's value chain is the flow of activities that extends from the first step (for example, identifying potential oil drilling sites) through the last (providing gasoline to consumers). Each step adds value to the one that precedes it.

  Value chains are dynamic. By eliminating intermediaries and facilitating business-to-business and business-to-customer linkages, the digital world is turning traditional value chains on their heads. As an organization evolves, it expands and contracts its scope. However, if you freeze-frame your organization at a moment in time, it is occupying a defined space in its industry. Markets serve as the right-hand boundary of your place in this value chain.

- *Suppliers and suppliers' suppliers.* Suppliers, who represent the left-hand boundary of your organization's position in its value chain, provide the raw material, components, and goods that go into your products and services. They, in turn, may have suppliers.

- *Resource providers,* which include:

    ➤ Schools, companies, and agencies that provide workers.

    ➤ Banks and venture capitalists that provide money.

    ➤ Academic institutions, research labs, and other companies that provide technology.

    ➤ Organizations to which your company or agency outsources functions such as manufacturing, distribution, accounting, market research, and human resource administration.

- *Competitors,* who meet the needs of the market with similar or substitute products and services.
- *Government,* which includes elected officials, courts, central banks, and regulatory agencies.
- *The economy,* which is not merely a function of government. It includes factors such as growth or contraction, inflation or deflation, financial optimism or fear, currency valuations, commodity prices, household income, and job creation.
- The *society and community,* which have interests in and concerns about quality of life, the environment, employment, and corporate citizenship.
- If your organization is part of a larger entity, your *corporate parent,* which influences a subsidiary through its strategy, culture, funding, mandates, and priorities.
- *Shareholders,* who provide funding and general direction in return for equity growth and dividends.

These universal variables may need to be supplemented by industry-specific external factors. For example, weather is a key variable for agriculture and leisure businesses.

Healthy interfaces with these external entities are built on a platform of understanding. For each of the factors defined above:

- How well do you understand the trends, strategy, needs, priorities, and processes of this variable?

- How well do you understand the ways in which this variable does and should influence you?
- How well do you understand the ways in which you do and should influence this variable?

The more deeply you understand these variables, the greater your appreciation for the water in which your organization swims.

These external variables are addressed in more depth in Chapter 2.

What Are the Structural Variables?

Four of the internal variables install a system, procedure, or mechanism for doing business. While these structural variables all need people to make them work, their primary contribution is to establish the floors and framing of the organizational house in which people live.

- *Business processes* are at the heart of your operations because they are the vehicles through which work gets done. Customer-touch processes include business development, order fulfillment, customer service, and product development. They are supported by internal processes such as hiring, planning, financial reporting, and resource allocation.

  While processes are only as good as the people who populate them, you cannot rely on exemplary talent to triumph over flawed systems. Business processes are structural because they provide the steps, protocols, and roles within which people do their jobs.

  The *business processes* variable is addressed in Chapter 5.
- *Goals* begin with the financial and nonfinancial targets for your overall business. These goals cascade through all organizational levels and ultimately describe the expectations of all individuals and teams. Goals become a management tool through a *measurement* system in which performance information is gathered, monitored, and used as the basis for problem solving and decision making.

  The *goals/measurement* variable is addressed in Chapter 6.

- *Information management* is the backbone of an organization. This variable includes your computer systems and the information they house, generate, correlate, and massage. It also includes the facts and perceptions that are in nondigital files and people's heads. In an organization managing this variable well, valuable information and learning are captured and made accessible in a *knowledge management* system. Those who need information on products, customers, processes, and capabilities can readily access it.

  The *information/knowledge management* variable is addressed in Chapter 9.

- *Organization structure* is the formal grouping of *roles* and *responsibilities* (for example, by function, product, customer, or geography) and the reporting hierarchy. It reflects the positional power in the organization and has a significant influence on workflows, day-to-day management, and career development.

  The *organization structure* variable is addressed in Chapter 10.

What Are the Human Variables?

The three human variables focus on the skills, motivation, and behaviors of people. They explore what people are able to do and what they actually do in their organizational lives.

- *Leadership* is the set of behaviors through which those with both positional power and influencing power steer the priorities, activities, and results of others in your organization. Leadership includes visioning, contextualizing, communicating, aligning, mobilizing, energizing, inspiring, enabling, rewarding, and developing.

  The *leadership* variable is addressed in Chapter 3.

- *Culture* includes the norms, folkways, practices, and unwritten rules that guide the way an organization conducts business. By examining your organization's culture, you gain insight into participation, risk orientation, innovation, interaction style, pace, and communication.

  The *culture* variable is addressed in Chapter 7.

- *Human capabilities* are the skills and knowledge of your workforce. Managerial skills, technical skills, and physical skills are the lifeblood of even the most automated operations. This variable also includes the individual values that support or inhibit performance.
The *human capabilities* variable is addressed in Chapter 8.

What Are the Variables That Are Equally Structural and Human?

Two variables strike a balance between the human and structural dimensions.

- *Strategy* is the framework of choices that define the nature and direction of your organization. Your strategy should answer these questions:

  1. What values and beliefs will drive our decisions and culture?
  2. What products/services will we offer?
  3. What markets/customers will we serve?
  4. What will make us successful?
  5. What results will we achieve?

  Strategy defines your organization's place in the economy and society. It is the variable that defines the "what" of your organization. The other eight internal variables are components of the "how."
  The structural dimension of strategy is the product decisions, market decisions, and goals that define the boundaries within which you conduct business. The human dimension is the vision that guides those decisions and steers your organization to their implementation.
  The *strategy* variable is addressed in Chapter 4.

- *Issue resolution* is the way in which you and your colleagues identify concerns, set priorities, solve problems, make decisions, and develop and implement plans. Issues may be current or future and present threats or opportunities. As issues surface in each of the other variables (for example, business process issues, organization structure issues, culture issues, capability issues), world-class organizations effectively and efficiently resolve them.

The structural aspect of *issue resolution* is comprised of the steps people follow and the templates they use when addressing their concerns. The human dimension is the analytical and creative thinking that has to flow through those steps and the nature and extent of participation in each step.

The *issue resolution* variable is addressed in Chapter 11.

The overarching internal variable questions are:

- Do you understand how each of these factors influences the performance of your organization?
- Do you know how you are performing in each of these areas?
- Do you know which of these factors represent the most significant current and future threats and opportunities?

Each chapter has a detailed self-assessment that should enable you to answer yes to each of these questions.

■ TAKING A HOLISTIC VIEW

As Figure 1.2 shows, these variables, like the organs in the body or the components of a bicycle, do not exist in isolation.

To resolve almost every complex issue, you must address more than one variable. Furthermore, the installation of any significant change requires managing multiple variables.

For example, the executives of a hotel chain may go off to the mountain and come down with the tablets of a new *strategy* that places their future focus on the business traveler. This new vision will not be successfully implemented without changes to *business processes* (for example, check-in/out, messaging), *human capabilities* (for example, meeting planning, customer service), and *culture* (for example, emphasis on speed, establishing decision-making authority at the customer contact point).

You cannot effectively address *organization structure* without examining the *strategy* and *business processes* that structure should support. You cannot change *culture* without developing

Compartmental View   Integrated View

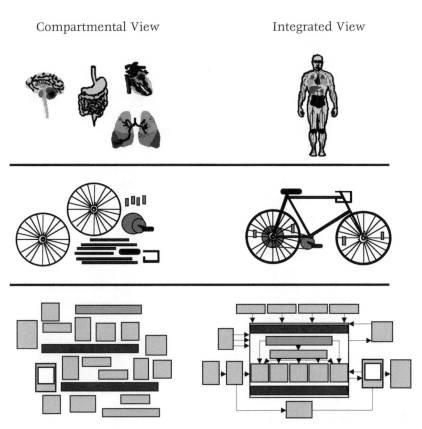

Figure 1.2 The Compartmental View and the Integrated View

human capabilities. You cannot formulate or implement *strategy* without *leadership.* The key to successful change is the *identification and integration of the relevant variables.*

The sequence and integration of variables are addressed in Chapter 12.

■ HOW CAN WE IMPROVE PERFORMANCE?

Executives in healthy organizations have learned a number of lessons from the Enterprise Model's holistic view of performance:

- The first step on the road to performance improvement is recognizing the external and internal variables and the role played by each.
- You can only achieve strategic results—increased shareholder value, growth in revenue and return, an enhanced brand—and operational results—increased quality, reduced cost, reduced cycle time—through the management of these variables.
- Most improvements require the integrated treatment of more than one variable. An enterprise is a system, not a collection of independent components.
- The variables are more than treatments for an existing disease. Like people who address elevated cholesterol levels before they lead to heart problems, world-class executives continuously assess each variable and address deficiencies before they become issues that affect their financial results.
- Organizations should have regular comprehensive physical exams that diagnose each factor that affects organizational health. Address weaknesses within the context of the other factors, ensuring that the treatment does not have side effects that are worse than the disease.
- Executives should manage all of the variables that can impact the outcome of a change initiative.

People have different health goals. Some are striving for longevity. Others simply want to be strong for whatever period of time they have on the planet. Some want to accomplish something athletically. Others see physical and mental health as part of a spiritual journey. Some just want to look good.

Similarly, organizations have different definitions of health. For some, the sole goal is increasing shareholder value. For others, it is to grow to a certain size. For some, it is doing something meaningful and lasting for the earth and its inhabitants. For others, it is providing a place in which employees can fulfill their intellectual and/or financial dreams. Some just want to look good.

Managing organizational health, like managing physical and mental health, requires a major commitment of time. However, there is no investment that has a higher potential return.

■ NOTE

1. For an earlier and less comprehensive version of the Enterprise Model, see the systems model in Geary Rummler and Alan Brache, *Improving Performance: How to Manage the White Space on the Organization Chart* (San Francisco: Jossey-Bass, 1995).

Chapter 2

Understanding the External Business Environment

Martin Althen appears to have things under control. The president of Sumpter Diagnostics, a chain of medical testing laboratories that serve doctors and hospitals, has an office that looks like the cockpit of a space shuttle. Displayed as dials in an instrument panel, he has measures of sales, profit, test quality, technician productivity, cost per lab and per test, test result turnaround time, and patient wait time. He is proud of the fact that, in spite of Sumpter's growth, he visits every one of the 25 labs every quarter and knows at least 80 percent of the employees by name.

However, Martin still does not think he has his finger fully on Sumpter's pulse. He has not been sleeping well lately because:

- Demand fluctuates widely and, because his overhead is mostly fixed, his profitability varies with it.
- The volume and types of tests change without warning and his labs find themselves with too many test kits for some diagnostics and too few for others. Training technicians in new procedures drains precious time and money.
- Sumpter routinely loses valued, long-term, apparently satisfied customers, especially health maintenance organizations. Martin does not know why.
- Government and private insurance claim documentation requirements appear to change daily.
- He continually hears about advances in testing technology but does not have the time to explore them.
- Good technicians do not remain with Sumpter nearly as long as they used to. Replacing them is increasingly difficult.

15

Martin is a participative executive. He spends most of each day discussing these issues in meetings with his headquarters team and with his lab managers in the field. These meetings are cathartic, but Martin is rarely satisfied with the decisions. Thinking that he might be the problem, he has deliberately excluded himself from the membership of many of the teams he has formed to address some of the key issues. These teams meet regularly, but appear to be little more than debating forums in which theories abound and nothing happens. When decisions are made, they seem to be based solely on the anecdotal experience of the more assertive team members.

Martin has good intentions and runs a pretty tight ship. However, he is buffeted by the winds of change. He is too frequently surprised by developments in his industry. His approach to issues tends to be internally focused. He does not have the external intelligence upon which to base decisions. He needs to better understand his environment.

Good physicians and psychologists need context. Before probing your inner person, they want to understand the environment in which you function. What is your work setting? (Do you work in a sealed office tower? a store? your home? on airplanes? at construction sites?) What are your job responsibilities and what demands do they put on you? How would you describe your home surroundings? What pressures are you under on the home front? At both work and nonwork locations, with whom do you interact regularly and what is the format/nature of those interactions? What are your extracurricular pursuits? Because physical and mental health are significantly influenced by external factors, doctors cannot treat your "whole person" without understanding the environment in which you function.

Similarly, you need to understand the context within which your business operates. Your external business environment includes both variables on which you have little or no influence (for example, interest rates, trade policies, the price of raw materials) as well as those that have resulted from your choices (for example, the markets you serve, your alliance partners, the sources of your funding). Before you can understand and improve the internal variables, you need to understand the milieu that is depicted in Figure 2.1.

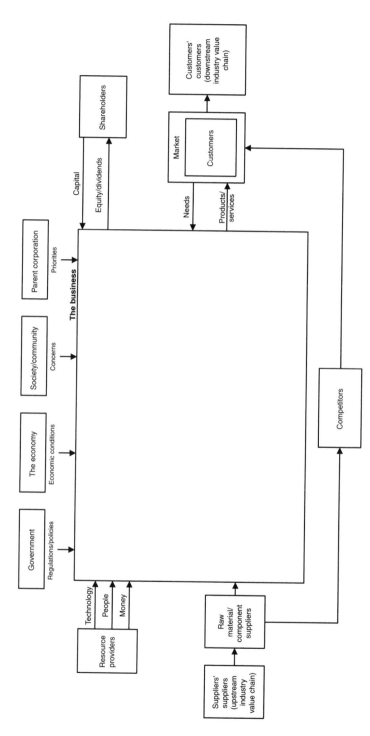

Figure 2.1 The Enterprise Model's External Variables

■ WHAT IS YOUR INDUSTRY'S VALUE CHAIN?

Let us begin by positioning your organization in what has become known as its "value chain" or "supply chain." The concept behind a value chain is that there are a number of links between the first and last commercial transactions in your industry. In each step, value is added and financial worth is increased. For example, a simplified value chain of the oil business is shown in Figure 2.2.

A company may participate in the entire value chain, as ExxonMobil does in the oil business. Other companies may participate in only a few steps (for example, Hess) or in just one step (for example, Colonial Pipeline).

Executives, particularly those who have spent their entire careers in mature industries, often fall into the trap of defining their value chain in historic terms that are out of touch with today's reality. Information technology and globalization are redefining and eliminating the links in traditional value chains. Value chains are being revolutionized by "disintermediation," in which steps—and those who participate in them—are being removed from the equation. If you can buy a customized computer on the Internet from Dell, and have Dell service it after the sale, you do not need a retail store. If you can buy and sell used items on eBay, you do not need the classified ads in your local newspaper. If, with three clicks of a button, cnn.com will give you the current and forecasted weather for any place in the world, in real time, on your wireless device, for free, you do not need a cable weather channel.

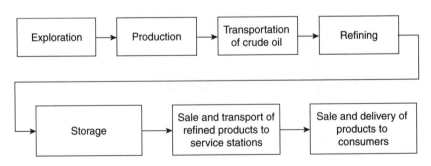

Figure 2.2 Basic Value Chain of the Petroleum Industry

On the other hand, the value chain may now include new players—"infomediaries"—who guide us to the information and services we need. Browsers such as Netscape and Microsoft Explorer and portals such as Yahoo! and Lycos are in some cases essential links in the chain that connects buyers to sellers. There are services, such as realtor.com (real estate) and quotesmith.com (insurance) that will direct a buyer to appropriate product or service providers and enable the buyer to comparison shop. Bots, such as MySimon and PriceSCAN, will find the lowest price for a given product. Electronic trading networks like ChemConnect (for chemicals, plastics, and industrial gases) and NECX (for electronics) serve as virtual marketplaces for business-to-business buyers and sellers.

Secondly, the advent of outsourcing has enabled companies to focus on the steps in the value chain that play to their strengths. Niche players no longer suffer from their lack of participation in the surrounding steps. In addition to administrative functions, many companies now outsource functions that have historically been considered core, such as research and development, manufacturing, and distribution. For example, Nike has decided that the manufacturing of its athletic shoes is not a competitive advantage, so it outsources that function, enabling it to focus its energies on market research, design, and marketing. Flextronics is a multibillion-dollar company that does not only contract manufacturing but also contract design for Motorola, Microsoft, Siemens, Ericsson, and Bosch.

Prahalad and Hamel[1] have described successful companies as those that not only excel at their "core competencies" but also "reinvent their industries." The creative definition of the future value chain is an essential part of strategy formulation.

■ WHAT DETERMINES SUCCESS IN YOUR PART OF THE VALUE CHAIN?

Once you establish your value chain, your executive team should agree on the Critical Success Factors (CSFs) in each step in that chain. CSFs are the variables that make or break anyone who chooses to play in the industry.

For example, the CSFs in the "exploration" step of the oil value chain include:

- Expertise in conducting geological surveys.
- Expertise in the acquisition of land/water drilling rights.
- Ability to secure quick financing.
- Ability to get crews and equipment up and running quickly.
- Ability to efficiently and effectively make "proceed/do not proceed" decisions.
- Ability to absorb the financial losses from nonproducing or low-producing wells.

The ante for any player in the exploration game is basic competence in each of these areas. The winners are those companies that are "best of breed" in one or more of these CSFs and at parity with their competitors in the others.

➤ SELF-ASSESSMENT QUESTIONS

➤ *In what value chain do we participate? (In other words, what industry are we in?)*

➤ *What are the current steps in that value chain?*

➤ *In which steps in the value chain do we currently participate?*

➤ *What are the likely future steps in that value chain? (You may want to create more than one possible future scenario.)*

➤ *Which future steps present the greatest opportunities, or "profit zones."?[2]*

➤ *What are the Critical Success Factors in each step in the likely future value chain?*

➤ *What is our current competitive position (competitive advantage, competitive disadvantage, parity) in terms of each Critical Success Factor?*

During strategy formulation, discussed in Chapter 4, executives should use the answers to these questions as the platform for carving out the portion of the future value chain in which they will participate. Then, they should identify the Critical

Success Factors in which they will maintain, establish, or extend a competitive advantage. During strategy implementation, executives design and oversee the deployment of actions to play in the appropriate steps in the value chain, establish the desired competitive advantages, and ensure parity in the other Critical Success Factor areas.

Without an understanding of the value chain, strategy is a shot in the dark.

■ WHO ARE YOUR MARKETS AND CUSTOMERS?

Once you have defined your value chain and positioned your business in the chain, you should solidify your understanding of the players in the boxes immediately to your right and left. To your right are your markets and, within those markets, the customers you currently serve. If you are not serving end users (typically called "consumers"), you also need to understand your customers' customers.

For example, Purina needs to understand not only the needs of its customers (the stores that sell its pet food products) but also the pet owners (and the pets) to whom its customers sell. Life Fitness, a provider of exercise equipment, needs to understand not only health clubs, hotels, and sporting goods stores but also the needs and buying criteria of people who exercise.

A central part of strategy development is determining the markets you will and will not serve. The better you understand your downstream value chain and how it adds value to the end user—even if there are steps in between—the greater your potential for success.

For example, I facilitated a session in which a rail freight company's executives met with their counterparts from a number of their key customers. We used the value chain as the foundation for discussion, analysis, and action planning. Our guiding question: How can we (the rail company) better help you (the rail company's customers) meet the needs of your customers? This exercise (1) strengthened the partnership between the rail company and its customers, (2) deepened the rail company's understanding of its customers' needs, (3) helped the customers better understand *their* customers' needs, and, perhaps most significantly, (4) generated additional business opportunities for the rail company. As a result of this meeting, the rail company began meeting a variety of its customers' packaging, storage, and distribution needs. Without straying beyond its competencies or strategy, it moved both upstream and downstream from its traditional position in the rail transportation portion of the value chain.

➤ **SELF-ASSESSMENT QUESTIONS**

➤ *What market(s) do we currently serve?*
➤ *What customers do we currently serve within this/these market(s)?*
➤ *What market(s) could we potentially serve?*
➤ *What customers could we potentially serve within these markets?*
➤ *What are the primary needs of our current and potential customers?*
➤ *Who are our customers' customers? Which of their needs do our customers meet? What drives their buying behavior?*
➤ *Do our customers' customers have any needs that we could meet directly? What would be the consequences of going directly to our customers' customers? Are there ways in which we could partner with our customers to meet their customers' needs?*
➤ *What are the strategies of our current and potential customers?*
➤ *Who do our customers see as our competitors?*
➤ *What do our customers see as our competitive advantages and disadvantages?*
➤ *In what ways could our customers become competitors?*
➤ *What are our primary customer threats and opportunities?*

As you develop your strategy, you can use the answers to these questions as the basis for (1) defining the market(s) in which you will compete, (2) targeting customers within those markets, (3) determining the range of customer needs you will meet, and (4) ensuring that you have a solid competitive advantage.

■ WHO ARE YOUR SUPPLIERS?

To the left of a business in its value chain are its suppliers. Hallmark needs paper for its greeting cards. Volvo needs aluminum for its cars. Marriott needs cleaning equipment and supplies. In many cases, suppliers also have suppliers. Compaq Computer gets its chips from Intel, which in turn gets silicon, gold, copper, and fabrication equipment from its suppliers. While your understanding of the downstream (market and customer) links in your value chain is paramount, you also have to be aware of the influence wielded by your suppliers and their suppliers in the upstream value chain.

➤ SELF-ASSESSMENT QUESTIONS

➤ *Who are our suppliers? Who are our potential suppliers?*
➤ *What influence do our suppliers have on our effectiveness? on our efficiency?*
➤ *Who are our suppliers' suppliers and what influence do they have on our business?*
➤ *What are the strategies of our key suppliers?*
➤ *In what ways could our suppliers become our competitors?*
➤ *What are our primary supplier threats and opportunities?*

During strategy formulation, executives determine what role suppliers will play, the kinds of partnerships they want to establish with suppliers, the number of supplier relationships they want to manage, and what actions they will take to ensure that suppliers do not become competitors.

■ WHO ARE YOUR RESOURCE PROVIDERS?

Another species of supplier is different enough to warrant its own category. Resource providers do not provide the tangible materials or components that go into your product, but they provide:

- The money that fuels your growth.
- The people that perform your work.
- The technology that supports your processes.
- Your noncore functions.

Your funding may come from a bank, a venture capitalist, or a corporate parent. Your people may come from domestic universities, local competitors, or other countries. Your technology may come from hardware and software developers or research labs. You may have some or all of your back-office functions (for example, finance, human resources, information systems, facilities management) and even nonstrategic line functions (for example, marketing, manufacturing, distribution) performed by firms that specialize in these areas.

As part of your business context, you need to understand your relationships with these providers, the influence you have on them, and the influence they have on you.

> ## ➤ SELF-ASSESSMENT QUESTIONS
>
> ➤ *Who are our resource providers? Who are our potential resource providers?*
> ➤ *What influence do our resource providers have on our effectiveness? on our efficiency?*
> ➤ *What are the strategies of our resource providers?*
> ➤ *What are our primary resource provider threats and opportunities?*

Decisions regarding sources of funding, people, technology, and noncore functions are part of strategy formulation. The processes for obtaining money, people, technology, and outsource partners are part of strategy implementation.

■ WHO ARE YOUR COMPETITORS?

Your external environment also includes the three types of companies with which you compete:

- *Direct competitors* offer a product that is in the same category as yours. If you work for Southwest Airlines, which sells air transportation, American Airlines is a direct competitor.
- *Indirect competitors* meet the same need in a different way. Greyhound sells bus transportation to many of the same markets and destinations as Southwest.
- *Root need competitors* eliminate your product or service from the equation by addressing the need that lies beneath the need you meet. AT&T Solutions sells videoconferencing facilities and services that eliminate the need for some business travel that might otherwise be taken on Southwest.

Defining your competitors and competitive advantages is a central dimension of strategy formulation. The broader your understanding of current and potential competitors, the stronger the foundation supporting your strategy.

➤ SELF-ASSESSMENT QUESTIONS

➤ *Who are our direct competitors? our indirect competitors? our root need competitors?*

➤ *Who are our potential competitors?*

➤ *What are the strategies of our competitors?*

➤ *What are our primary competitive threats and opportunities?*

■ WHO ARE YOUR SHAREHOLDERS?

Shareholders are the owners of the business. If your business is a publicly or privately held company, the shareholders are those who own stock. If your business is a division or subsidiary, your shareholder is the parent corporation and, ultimately, the owners of that parent. If you work for a government agency, your shareholders are taxpayers.

Shareholders may or may not be interested in the daily operations of your company. They usually are interested in your business strategy. They are always interested in the returns—be it in the form of cash, dividends, or appreciation—on their investment in your company.

> ## ➤ SELF-ASSESSMENT QUESTIONS
>
> ➤ *Who are our shareholders?*
> ➤ *What are our shareholders' financial goals for our business?*
> ➤ *What are our shareholders' nonfinancial goals for our business?*
> ➤ *What voice do our shareholders expect to have in our strategy? What strategic information do our shareholders need?*
> ➤ *What operational information do our shareholders need?*
> ➤ *What are our primary shareholder threats and opportunities?*

■ WHAT ARE YOUR OTHER EXTERNAL INFLUENCES?

The four remaining external variables are:

- *Government,* which exerts two types of influence. One is through its laws and regulations. For example, chemical companies are heavily influenced by air and water cleanliness regulations. Airlines have to conform to air safety regulations. Pharmaceutical companies must follow drug approval regulations and operate within patent protection laws. Food companies have to follow inspection regulations. All companies have to conform to disabled worker discrimination laws and regulations.

  The second government influence is through its policies and priorities. For example, an administration's trade policies, monetary policies, and antitrust policies influence most businesses.
- *The economy,* which is much more than the by-product of government policies. It is affected by factors such as com-

pany productivity and profitability, stock market performance, political stability, and consumer confidence. It exerts influence on a business through interest rates, unemployment rates, growth rates, and exchange rates.

- *Society/community.* Smokestack manufacturing companies are influenced by environmental advocacy groups. Clothing companies are influenced by dress norms and fashion preferences. All companies are subject to pressure from citizen groups that want to control the appearance of, traffic in, and employment opportunities in their communities.
- *Parent corporation.* A business owned by a larger enterprise is influenced by the strategy, priorities, culture, initiatives, and financial well-being of its parent.

In addition to these generic variables, certain industries are influenced by other external factors. In agriculture, weather is a major variable. In some industries, trade groups and consumer associations are powerful. For example, the American Medical Association and American Association of Retired Persons are influential in the U.S. health care industry. In some industries, like automotive and transportation, unions are powerful external forces as well as internal constituencies.

➤ SELF-ASSESSMENT QUESTIONS

➤ *What are our primary governmental influences?*
➤ *What are our primary economic influences?*
➤ *What are our primary society/community influences?*
➤ *If we have a parent corporation, what are its primary influences?*
➤ *What are our other external influences?*

For each of these variables:

➤ *What is the current state of the influence being exerted by this variable?*
➤ *What is the potential future influence?*
➤ *How does this variable impact our effectiveness? our efficiency?*
➤ *What are the primary threats and opportunities in this variable?*

■ WHAT IS THE PROCESS FOR ADDRESSING THE EXTERNAL VARIABLES?

To proactively manage your external environment:

1. *Define your current and likely future value chain.* Determine the flow of your industry and your current position in it. (This position may change as a by-product of your strategy deliberations, but you should begin by capturing the current situation.) Focus particularly on the definition of your customers and suppliers. Then, polish your crystal ball and determine what you see as the value chain of the future.

   Martin Althen, the beleaguered Sumpter Diagnostics president introduced at the beginning of this chapter, has allowed himself to be victimized by his environment. He has begun to recognize that internal controls and meetings are not a substitute for external understanding. As business-people without a manufacturing orientation, he and his executive team had never thought of being part of a value chain. When at last they did, they found tremendous value in defining the medical testing industry in those terms. For example, they had a healthy debate about whether their primary customers were the doctors that requested tests, the patients, the insurance companies, or all three. Their discussion of the evolution of the value chain forced an unprecedented depth of thinking and foresight.

2. *Identify your competitors, resource providers, and other external variables.* Using the six sets of Self-Assessment Questions that appear above, identify the environmental factors that have the greatest influence on your business.

   The Sumpter team:

   ➤ **Identified their primary competitors today and their most formidable emerging competitors.**

   ➤ **Thought for the first time about the labor market and its influence on their ability to attract first-class technicians.**

➤ Identified alternative funding sources.

➤ Highlighted the technological developments that influenced Sumpter's business.

➤ Documented the government regulations and policies that most influenced them and realized that they could, by joining with existing health care provider associations and lobbying entities, exert much more influence than they had historically.

➤ Identified the economic and societal variables that they could not influence but needed to factor into their decision making.

3. *Establish an environmental monitoring system.*

As the opening paragraph indicates, Martin was a measurement junkie. However, he realized that all of his tracking was against *internal* metrics. He tasked a team with developing an environmental monitoring system. The system they developed captures:

➤ Health care trends.

➤ Competitor trends.

➤ Insurance coverage and claim-processing trends.

➤ Technological trends.

➤ Legislative/regulatory trends.

➤ Economic trends.

They also designed and installed a customer satisfaction system that enabled them to understand the reasons for attrition and the early warning indicators that signal a customer's likely intent to reduce or cease the use of Sumpter's services.

4. *Identify the critical external issues facing your organization.* Based on your environmental monitoring, determine your current and future external threats and opportunities. The strategic issues can be addressed as part of the process outlined in Chapter 4. The tactical issues can be addressed using the tools presented in Chapter 11.

The Sumpter executive team identified their most critical external issues as:

➤ The growing number of on-premises labs owned and operated by health maintenance organizations and hospitals.
➤ The trend toward at-home test kits.
➤ The trend toward more preventive testing.
➤ The exponential increase in DNA-based testing for both forensic and health purposes.
➤ The shortage of qualified lab technicians.
➤ The lowering of fees insurance companies are willing to pay for standard lab tests.
➤ The increasing regulatory oversight of all health care.

The first step in your performance improvement journey is deepening your understanding of the controllable and uncontrollable variables in the environment in which your organization conducts business. Your position in that environment and your definition of how you will succeed in that environment are central components of your strategy, which is the subject of Chapter 4. As Step 3 above indicates, your organization needs to supplement internal performance monitoring with external environment tracking; Chapter 6 includes both dimensions in its treatment of goal setting and measurement.

■ NOTES

1. C.K. Prahalad and G. Hamel, *Competing for the Future* (Boston: Harvard Business School Press, 1994).
2. A.J. Slywotzky and D.J. Morrison, *The Profit Zone: How Strategic Business Design Will Lead You to Tomorrow's Profits* (New York: Times Business, 1997).

Chapter 3

Leading the Enterprise

On paper, Westbrook Plastics, a contract-manufacturing firm, appears to have the infrastructure of a solid company. Revenue and profit growth are unspectacular but steady. The balance sheet is clean. Employee retention exceeds industry standards. Unlike most of its competitors, the company has never had a major safety or environmental incident.

However, there is rot under the floorboards:

- Westbrook has not had a successful new product launch in eight years.
- The company relies on its "good old boy" network of customers. Unlike their predecessors, young purchasing and manufacturing managers have not heard of Westbrook.
- Sales people rarely land a new big-name account. When they do, it tends to result in a "one-off" order as opposed to a long-term relationship.
- The brand has lost its luster and even its meaning. As a private label manufacturer, Westbrook has never been a household name; however, it had been seen as the premier player in its niche: heavy-duty extruded plastic products for the lawn care, outdoor furniture, and do-it-yourself markets. As it has strayed from that niche, its image has become muddy. Bored by the traditional product lines, the former CEO got Westbrook into specialized applications such as medical devices, office supplies, and appliances. Those forays have put the company up against

much stronger competition, confused its traditional customers, and resulted in atrophy of the core business.
- The board ultimately ousted the CEO who had taken them into the new businesses. His interim successor was the senior vice president of operations, who drove out waste, upgraded systems, and streamlined processes but did little to reestablish historic competitive advantages or energize the company. Upon his retirement, a young outsider with a marketing background replaced him. During her 15 months in the job, she has put some slick promotional programs in place, but has failed to focus the fragmented activities or put the company on a solid growth trajectory.
- Westbrook has no presence on the Internet.
- While Westbrook's compensation packages are competitive and locations are desirable, it attracts second-tier sales, engineering, and manufacturing talent. Low employee turnover is seen by many not as a strength but as part of Westbrook's malaise.
- The Westbrook culture is best described as technically competent and customer focused, but tired, inbred, critical, innovation averse, slow, and passionless.

Westbrook has a panoply of needs. It has strategy issues, culture issues, technology issues, and capability issues. However, underlying all of them is a deficiency in leadership.

While all members of a sports team are important, an owner can build a franchise around a single player. Similarly, all of your Enterprise Model variables are critical, but you can build your franchise around talented leadership. A comprehensive set of goals, well-oiled business processes, state-of-the-art systems, and skilled people can not compensate for weak leadership. On the other hand, a talented individual can lead an organization to success in spite of shortcomings in other areas. As its placement in the Enterprise Model suggests, the *leadership* variable is "first among equals."

■ WHAT IS LEADERSHIP?

Leadership is setting a direction and motivating people to go in that direction. It includes:

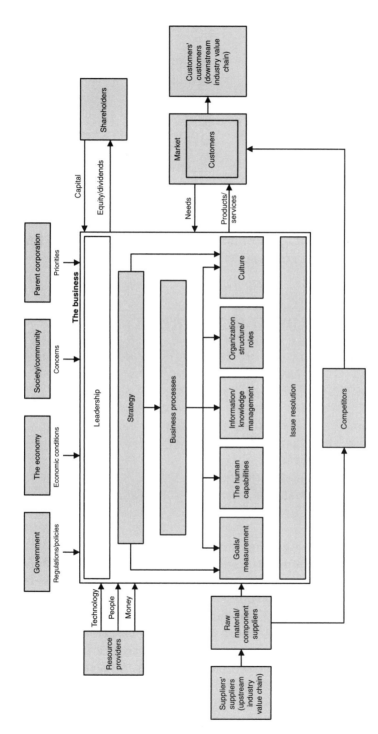

Figure 3.1 The Position of Leadership in the Enterprise Model

- Visioning.
- Communicating.
- Aligning.
- Mobilizing.
- Cheerleading.
- Enabling.
- Developing.

- Contextualizing.
- Inspiring.
- Energizing.
- Risk taking.
- Dramatizing.
- Rewarding.
- Role modeling.

While leadership manifests itself in behaviors, it is rooted as much in personality as in decisions and actions. It is as much about *how* things are done as *what* things are done.

■ WHY IS LEADERSHIP IMPORTANT?

Without leadership, an organization is unlikely to have a clear direction. Or, it may have a direction that is unambiguous but does not:

- Extend beyond the obvious opportunities.
- Realize the organization's full potential.
- Excite the market.
- Frighten the competition.
- Stimulate investors.
- Energize employees.

Nobody disputes the impact that culture (the subject of Chapter 7) has on performance. Culture spawns or stifles innovation, stimulates or discourages above-and-beyond levels of customer service, and reinforces or punishes risk taking. The single most powerful determinant of an organization's culture is the behavior of its leaders. If the chief executive and other leaders are entrepreneurial, the culture tends to be entrepreneurial. If a leader will not pass judgment on a recommendation that is not backed up by facts, that bias tends to permeate the ranks. Organizations in which a leader prefers voice mail to e-mail tend to communicate via voice mail.

An organization without strong leadership can grow, at least in the short run. It can be profitable. It can enjoy a solid reputation. However, it lacks vitality. It does not tend to attract the best and the brightest. It rarely breaks new ground. It does not inspire people inside or outside its doors.

■ WHAT DO LEADERS DO?

Leaders create distinct and compelling visions. When leaders look at their business, they:

- *See opportunities that are beyond others' scope.* A leader asks, "Could we contribute to global understanding and build a profitable business by establishing an all-news channel that meets people's need for current event information when and where they want it?" Those who thought Ted Turner picked too narrow a niche in 1980 have since been humbled by the Fishing Channel and the Game Show Network. Then there are those 24/7 webcams in dormitory rooms . . .
- *See things in a different way.* A leader asks, "Rather than making money by selling products, could we make money by creating a 'virtual marketplace' that brings together buyers and sellers?" Only a visionary could be the first to see that his organization could be more successful as a creator of a business space than by selling traditional products or services.

  Tommy Hilfiger sells clothing. Virgin's Richard Branson sells air transportation, soda, and recorded music. However, the real product they are both selling is their brand. Herb Kelleher of Southwest Airlines sees "acting small" as the path to growth and was able to create a more enjoyable customer experience by offering *less* service.
- *See novel uses for traditional products.* A leader learns that there are no more permits for billboards and sees a steady parade of cars traveling along certain highways and streets. (The drivers may be talking on their cell phones, eating lunch, and reading their e-mail, but they occasionally look at the road.) He says, "I would bet that many drivers would be willing, for a monthly fee, to have advertising put on

their cars. And I predict that many companies would jump at the chance to promote their products that way."

The turnaround of Apple in 1999 and 2000 can be attributed in large measure to Steve Jobs's vision of personal computers as works of art.

■ *Synthesize what others see as discrete needs or pieces of information.* A leader asks, "Could we develop a single, affordable, user-friendly wireless device that serves the needs currently being addressed by telephones, computers, schedule planners, address books, and pagers?"

A leader sees the burgeoning popularity of mutual funds, heightened interest in work-life balance, increased wealth, and longer life spans and asks, "Could we develop a portfolio of '40 years of retirement' funds for people at different levels of risk tolerance?"

The need for packaged synthesis has created a cottage industry of futurists in which the Alvin Tofflers, John Naisbetts, and Watts Wackers thrive.

Couldn't any creative person laboring in the trenches of marketing, research, or a university possess this "visioning" ability? Yes. However, leaders also have the ability to transform visions into reality. They:

■ *Communicate* the "what" and "why" of the vision to those who can operationalize it.
■ *Mobilize* the resources that can operationalize the vision.
■ *Demonstrate an infectious passion* for the vision.
■ *Motivate* the most talented people to pursue the vision, even when it means personal sacrifice (for example, financial risk, additional work hours, more travel, increased stress).
■ *Generate commitment,* rather than wielding the club of compliance.
■ *Serve as the chief cheerleader* for the vision, both inside and outside the organization.
■ *Reward* accomplishments on the way to implementing the vision.
■ *Take calculated risks* that are necessary for full implementation of the vision.

- *Establish risk boundaries* that provide implementers a sufficiently expansive arena in which they can stick their neck out without being punished.
- *Remove barriers*—political, financial, structural, and cultural—to implementing the vision.
- *Develop people,* enabling them to perform at unprecedented levels on current and future projects.
- *Reenergize* the implementers when they fall into the "it is hopeless" troughs that are part of any major change.
- *Create a "lessons-learned" environment* in which failures, as well as successes, enable the organization to do better next time.
- *Are unwavering and tireless* in pursuit of the vision.
- *Role model* behaviors that embody the vision.
- *Take personal responsibility* for the success or failure of the vision.

Leaders do not simply champion new products or services. They display the same vision and characteristics when leading an acquisition, a restructuring, or a brand repositioning. World-class leaders can stand up to the challenge of successfully implementing an unpopular or humbling action, like downsizing, withdrawing from a market, or managing the fallout from a highly publicized defective product.

■ WHAT ROLE DOES COMMUNICATION PLAY?

A leader can lack the ability to take some of the actions listed above. However, one talent must be in the repertoire: communication. If you are unable to communicate your grand vision or your enthusiasm for its realization, you are unlikely to be an effective leader.

While there are many communications methods and styles, there is no substitute for the rallying cry. For example:

- John Young, former CEO of Hewlett-Packard, declared that there would be a tenfold reduction in field failure rate across all product lines. "10 X" became the benchmark that galvanized the organization.

- Herb Kelleher, CEO of Southwest Airlines, said that Southwest would have the lowest fares on all of its routes. That simple commitment established a clear, compelling direction. It is no coincidence that Southwest has the longest sustained profitability of any major airline. And, employees at all levels sure seem to have fun pursuing their goal.
- Bob Galvin, former CEO of Motorola, challenged employees in all areas—line and staff—to attain a goal of "Six Sigma" performance. (Six Sigma is a statistical measure that equates to no more than 3.4 errors per million units or transactions, regardless of the product or service.) Six Sigma has become a quality mantra in Motorola and has spread to other companies.
- Jack Welch, former CEO of GE, said that every GE business unit would be either #1 or #2 in its market. There is no fuzz on that target.
- In some cases, the rallying cry also serves as a marketing tag line. For example:

  ➤ Compaq CEO Michael Capellas's "Everything to the Internet."

  ➤ Microsoft Chairman Bill Gates's and CEO Steve Ballmar's "Software as a service."

  ➤ PepsiCo's CEO Roger Enrico's plan to harness the power of its soft drink and snack brands around the "Power of One."

As these examples illustrate, effective rallying cries tend to be brief, catchy, a stretch, and anchored by a metric against which performance can be assessed.

■ HOW DOES LEADERSHIP DIFFER FROM MANAGEMENT (AND DOES IT MATTER)?

While a firm line of demarcation between leadership and management has little practical value, it is useful to explore the ways in which each contributes to success.

Management can be seen as the fundamentals of running a business. Good managers:

- Put streamlined business processes in place.
- Establish a workable organization structure.
- Establish clear roles and responsibilities.
- Develop performance standards, measure performance against those standards, and take action based on the measurement information.
- Solve operational problems or see that they are solved.
- Make operational decisions or see that they are made.
- Oversee the development and implementation of plans and budgets.
- Ensure that people get regular feedback.
- Create environments in which good performance is rewarded and substandard performance is not.
- Equip people with the skills to do their job.

You can see how this list differs from the behaviors, attributes, and skills described in "What Do Leaders Do?"

The wisdom dispensed by leadership pundits often leaves their audiences with the impression that true leaders are rare (which is true) and effective managers are a commodity (which is not true).

Many responsibilities require both leadership and management. Strategy formulation, for example, contains a visionary component that is the domain of leadership, as well as product/market priority setting, which is hard-core management. Successful product development demands, as George Bush the elder called it, "the vision thing," but also requires the nitty-gritty of market testing, economic modeling, and project management.

Many managers are not strong leaders. At least as many leaders are not strong managers. This should not be surprising, because the skills are different. Few renowned saxophone players are also first-rate guitarists.

An effective organization has both leaders and managers in positions that draw on their strengths. A leader develops the concept of a train, identifies the market for trains, and envisions where trains should go. Managers build trains, see that they run on time, and ensure that the rail transportation business makes money.

Would you rather have effective leaders or effective managers? Yes.

■ IS THERE ONE LEADERSHIP PROFILE?

While effective leaders tend to share the characteristics and roles listed above, they are not clones. They differ based on:

- *The type and maturity of the business.* A high-technology start-up company has different leadership needs than a large company in a mature industry. A global, multibusiness company puts a premium on different leadership skills than a domestic single-business company. Manufacturing plant leaders require a different orientation from those who lead research institutions, government bodies, and advertising agencies.

  A software company may need its leader to also play the role of "chief applications architect." An aerospace company may need its leader to serve as its "chief military sales officer." A hazardous chemical manufacturer may need its leader to also be its "chief public relations officer." A health maintenance organization's leader may also be "chief lobbyist." Nonleaders may specialize in application development, sales, and public relations. However, internal priorities and external stakeholders may demand that a CEO allocate a disproportionate amount of time to providing leadership in these areas, each of which requires unique skills.

- *The strategy of the business.* A company that is going to grow through global expansion may need leaders with experience in international operations and deal making. A company with a premium product may need a different type of leader than one in which success depends on being the low-cost producer. A company that is on the leading edge puts different demands on a leader than one pursuing a "fast-follower" strategy.

- *The style of the leader.* Effective leaders span the spectrum of personality types and interaction styles. See "Are Leaders Born or Made?" later in this chapter.

What leaders do in all of these situations—envision, energize, develop, communicate—is the same. However, *how* they go about it may differ considerably.

■ WHERE DO LEADERS SIT?

Leaders typically operate from a position of authority. They may be CEOs, presidents, division heads, or country managers. At a lower level, they may manage a store, a product line, a plant, or a department.

However, there are two types of leaders who do not have impressive titles and may not have any direct reports. One is *thought leaders,* who use brainpower, rather than position, as their platform. These individuals—who may be sales representatives, researchers, shop foremen, or staff people—forge a vision for their area or, in some cases, for the entire business. They use the power and passion of their ideas to energize people to follow that vision.

Jesus Christ, Mahatma Ghandi, Elizabeth Cady Stanton, Plato, Martin Luther King, and Peter Drucker never held political office, ran a major corporation, commanded troops, or had the benefit of great wealth. Their leadership, and ultimately their power, came from their ideas, their ability to communicate those ideas, and their embodiment of those ideas.

While thought leaders in organizations usually need the approval of those with more positional power, they become the driving forces for change.

A second type of person who can innovate, captivate, and motivate without being in a position of formal authority is the *performance leader.* This individual may not have impressive intellectual bandwidth or be a silver-tongued communicator. However, he or she, by dint of an outstanding individual contribution, sets a new standard and leads others to higher levels of performance.

- A field service representative who leaves the customer his home phone number and calls 24 hours after the repair to see if everything is okay is role modeling a behavior others can emulate.

- A project manager, on her own time, customizes a software program so that it facilitates juggling multiple simultaneous projects. When she shares that program with her peers, she is demonstrating performance leadership.
- A salesperson who sets up customer-networking forums can motivate others to do the same.
- An introverted quality analyst who, from the obscurity of his cubicle, repeatedly finds the causes of recurring problems—and inspires others to do so—is leading by example.

While thought and performance leaders may not be able to take all of the actions listed previously (for example, mobilizing resources, removing financial barriers), they are key tiles in an organization's leadership mosaic. Executives who are not strong leaders, but who are wise enough to recognize it, can use thought leaders and performance leaders to fill at least some of the gap.

■ WHAT DO LEADERS REQUIRE?

When leaders turn around, they need to see people behind them. Some organizations do not have a critical mass of people who are constitutionally able to follow even the most inspiring leader. Some people's leadership proclivities or aspirations serve as barriers to followership; they see potential leaders as competitors. Others, probably because of the failure of past change efforts, are too jaded to follow anyone anywhere. Others, most often because the culture has beaten them down, just do not have the energy.

Leaders also require infrastructure. Even in a "skunk works" environment, leaders can only deploy their vision through *goals, processes, information systems, structure,* and the other variables in the Enterprise Model.

■ ARE LEADERS BORN OR MADE?

Leadership is not present or absent. Some people simply have more innate leadership ability than others. A thoughtful review of the list of leadership behaviors in "What Do Leaders Do?" inevitably leads to the conclusion that some leadership behaviors can be developed and others cannot. Training and development can fill some of the gaps in people with innate leadership traits and instincts. It can also help develop some basic capabilities in people who are not natural leaders.

People who are not natural communicators can learn that skill. They may never be Demosthenes or Winston Churchill; however, they can be taught to use the power of words to inspire. Individuals can be taught to create challenging targets, establish risk boundaries, and remove barriers to project success. Potential leaders can master a piece of the motivation puzzle by learning what stimulates people and providing the right messages and incentives.

However, training cannot provide the complete package. No developmental experience—be it in the work setting, in a classroom, at an ashram, or on a mountain-climbing expedition—can implant vision, energy, or constancy of purpose. Nor can it inject the charisma gene that enables leaders to get people to commit, often on blind faith.

Training is only one developmental path. Leadership can also be nurtured through on-the-job coaching and mentoring. Sometimes, the best developmental experience is to be thrown into the deep end of the pool. An individual's leadership aptitude often remains undetected until he or she is given the opportunity to lead. When people are asked to manage a key initiative or handle a crisis, they may surface and develop leadership abilities that were not required by their previous jobs. When looking for potential leaders, nobody picked haberdasher Harry Truman out of the lineup.

Leaders do not fit a certain personality profile. Some are extroverts; others avoid the stage. Some are organized; some are lucky to have socks that match. Some shout; others whisper. Some like the high life; others are monastic. Some are kind; others are nasty. However, leaders do share some traits:

- They are willing to make enemies. (This is the reason most politicians are not leaders.)
- They command respect. That respect may be founded on the leader's vision, integrity, intelligence, or functional

skills (in closing big deals, for example, or sniffing out talent). There is no leadership without respect.
- They are focused on the end game. They do not allow anyone or anything to distract them from the result they want to achieve.

Here is a simple leadership test: What is the impact when an individual merely walks into a room? If his or her presence is immediately felt, if people look toward him or her, if people expect that something is about to happen, you are probably in the presence of leadership.

■ WHAT IS THE KEY INGREDIENT IN LEADERSHIP?

Some people maintain that communication is the key ingredient in the leadership recipe. Others think it is intelligence, be it raw or refined. Still others cite energy. While not discounting the importance of any of these attributes, I'd vote for *passion.* Passion requires deep-seated belief. It involves outward displays of zeal, intensity, and emotional (not just intellectual) commitment. Passion itself communicates, regardless of the words that are chosen. As a leadership trait, passion can often compensate for gaps in intelligence. Passion generates energy.

Leaders are like puppies; you never catch them sleeping.

■ WHAT ARE THE TYPICAL LEADERSHIP WEAKNESSES?

The most common organizational leadership shortcomings are:

- Having an imbalance in the leadership/management mix.
- Assuming that leadership will bubble up or knock on the door rather than emerge from a proactive leadership acquisition/development plan.
- Assuming that a visionary, inspiring CEO is all the leadership that is needed (in other words, failing to build a broad leadership base).

- Equating leadership with the personality cult that has formed around an individual. The attraction may be based on likability, talent, wit, or appearance, rather than leadership.
- Believing that increased power leads to increased leadership. (While individuals can rise to the occasion, leadership more frequently leads to power than the converse.)
- Failing to build followership.

➤ SELF-ASSESSMENT QUESTIONS

➤ *Are our organization's top executives "leaders," as defined previously?*

➤ *Given the business we are in, in what other areas does our organization most need leadership? In which product lines? In which functions? In which countries? Do we have leaders in these areas?*

➤ *Do we have "thought leaders" and "performance leaders" in the right places?*

➤ *Are thought leaders and performance leaders rewarded for playing a leadership role?*

➤ *Do we have a process for bringing in leaders from outside the organization?*

➤ *In which of the leadership areas described in "What Do Leaders Do?" are we strongest? In which are we weakest?*

➤ *Do we have processes and programs for developing leadership capabilities?*

➤ *Do we have followers?*

➤ *Do we have "managers," as defined above?*

➤ *When major change efforts fall short of expectations, how much of the cause is a leadership deficiency? management deficiency? other factors?*

➤ *When medium-impact projects fall short of expectations, how much of the cause is a leadership deficiency? a management deficiency? other factors?*

■ WHAT IS THE PROCESS FOR ADDRESSING THE LEADERSHIP VARIABLE?

To diagnose your organization's leadership and take necessary action:

1. *Identify the areas in which your organization most needs leadership.*

   The outside directors of Westbrook, the plastics company introduced at the beginning of this chapter, have known for some time that the company needs a more focused strategy, a more motivated workforce, and a different customer profile. Westbrook needs product leadership, market leadership, and technology leadership. The directors now recognize that these needs will not be met without stronger leadership in the CEO position and in four other key roles. They have decided to explore the matter further.

2. *Develop your organization's current leadership profile and identify the gaps between that profile and your needs.*

   The outside directors have discreetly audited Westbrook's leadership. They know the CEO firsthand. Assuming an activist role, they have collected information on the bench strength beneath her. They have concluded that the company's executives are competent managers. They are intelligent, ethical, hard working, relatively apolitical, and committed to Westbrook's success. However, they lack vision. They are not motivators. All but one of them—the head of business development—are weak communicators. None of them has those intangible qualities that inspire people to unite behind them and follow them into an exciting but uncertain future.

3. *Develop a short-term plan* that closes leadership gaps by some combination of:

   ➤ Establishing clear leadership expectations and consequences for the existing executives.

   ➤ Promoting individuals with demonstrated leadership into higher-impact positions.

   ➤ Recruiting leadership talent from outside the organization.

The outside board members are now ready to go public with their assessment and plan. They do not want a second CEO change in 15 months or to foster an environment of fear and rumors. Since leadership has not been raised as an issue before, and because the current executives have many positive qualities, they want to create an opportunity for them to step up to the challenge. So they will not replace the CEO or any of the other executives at this time.

Rather than raising the issue at a board meeting, they meet individually with the five executives in the positions upon which Westbrook's future success depends. During those meetings, they define the leadership gaps and provide each of them with clear expectations that must be met within the next six months. They realize that these individuals cannot get a leadership transplant in this period of time but can take some actions to demonstrate their potential. One of the expectations is the recruitment and fast-tracking of leadership talent from outside the organization.

4. *Fill the leadership pipeline* by:
   ➤ Identifying individuals with leadership traits.
   ➤ Closing leadership ability gaps in those with leadership traits.
   ➤ Cultivating basic leadership abilities in individuals without intrinsic leadership traits.

   The expectations the board gives to the CEO include the installation of a leadership development program. They leave its form up to the CEO and indicate that they will review her plan at the fourth-quarter board meeting.

Leadership is required in the development and implementation of each of the other components in the Enterprise Model. For example, without strong, enlightened leadership, an organization is unlikely to have a winning *strategy*, world-class *business processes,* fully developed *human capabilities,* or a healthy *culture.* As these boats are launched in the chapters that follow, you will see the necessity of having leaders at the helm and in the crow's nest.

Chapter 4

Creating Strategic Alignment

Ken Weymouth's head hurts. The CEO of Health Aid, a midsized pharmaceutical company specializing in over-the-counter and generic prescription medications, is cursed—and blessed—with options.

- The industry is consolidating. Conventional wisdom suggests that only a small number of companies will survive. Ken is not sure if that is true and, if so, if Health Aid has sufficient critical mass.
- Ken is aware of a number of acquisition opportunities but doubts his company's ability to absorb the financial impact of an acquisition. And he thinks that any of the potential acquirees would experience tissue rejection by the old guard in his management team.
- Some major shareholders are pressuring Ken to put Health Aid on the auction block. They do not think the company can remain successful at its current size. Nor do they think it could achieve sufficient mass through either organic growth or acquisitions of companies it could financially and culturally absorb. They think Health Aid would be attractive to a number of large firms.
- All of the big players in the industry have drug patents that are expiring. Regulatory authorities are likely to approve the sale of less potent versions of these medications on a nonprescription basis. All projections indicate that the companies that are first to market with less expensive over-the-counter versions will make a lot of money.

- International markets, in which Health Aid is a minor participant, appear to have tremendous potential for its existing products.
- The company does no business via e-commerce and has no links to the firms that sell medicine over the Internet.
- A number of Health Aid's most formidable competitors are reducing prices to buy market share.
- The growth in medical products and accessories is far greater than the growth in pharmaceuticals. While Health Aid has the sales expertise and distribution channels to get into this business, Ken has been resisting it.

Ken may need more research. He may need a consultant. He may need an epiphany. He may need a megadose of Health Aid's Pain-Away. But mostly he needs a strategy.

■ WHAT IS STRATEGY?

"Strategy" is a term that is overused and, as a result, has lost precision of meaning. During a random two-day visit to an organization, you are likely to hear references to marketing strategy, human resource strategy, customer retention strategy, Internet strategy, and telephone cost-management strategy.

"Strategic" is often, and inappropriately, used to describe:

- Something in the *top tier of priorities*. An operational (tactical) issue (for example, determining how to reverse the escalation of machine maintenance costs) can be more serious, and certainly more urgent, than a strategic issue (for example, deciding when and how to enter the China market).
- Something *big*. Selecting the location for the consolidated back-office operations—an operational decision—may have more financial and human impact than a strategic decision, such as determining whether a low-performing product line should be phased out or merely de-emphasized.
- Something *long term*. A strategic decision (for example, whether to respond to a request for proposal from a potential customer outside a target market) can be implemented and consume significant resources within a week. The

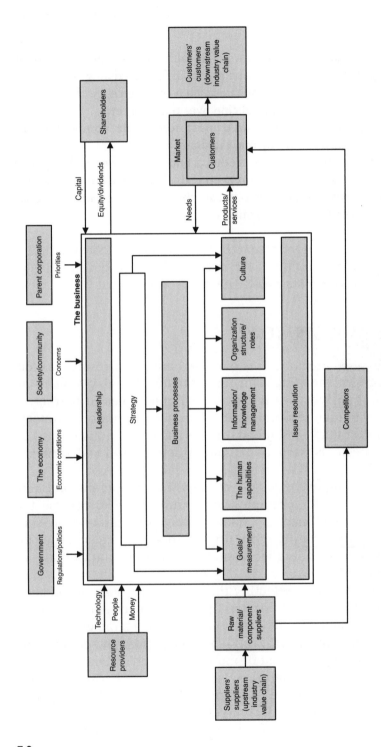

Figure 4.1 The Position of Strategy in the Enterprise Model

implementation of an operational decision (for example, installing a companywide customer database) can begin in four months and take a year.

A decision is not strategic by virtue of its size, weight, or timing; it is strategic because of its unique focus. *Strategy is the framework of choices that determine the nature and direction of an orga-nization.* A strategy positions a business—be it a company, division, agency, region, or department—in its external environment, defined in Chapter 2.

■ WHAT QUESTIONS SHOULD A STRATEGY ANSWER?

Regardless of the format or length of the document in which it appears, a strategy should answer these questions:

- What are our fundamental values and beliefs?
- How far into the future will we look?
- What products/services will we and will we not offer?
- What customer groups and geographic areas will we and will we not serve?
- What will fuel our growth?
- What products/services and markets represent our greatest potential and require the most significant investment?
- What competitive advantage(s) will cause us to succeed?
- What infrastructure and skills do we need to support our competitive advantage(s)?
- What financial and nonfinancial results will we achieve?

The answers to these questions must stand up to two reality tests:

- The viability test (Will it work?)
- The doability test (Can we implement it?)

■ WHY TAKE TIME TO FORMULATE STRATEGY?

Strategy provides the context for operational decisions. A good strategy—one that provides convincing answers to the questions listed previously—establishes the right boundaries and guidance for decisions regarding

- The type and quantity of people to hire.
- The content and thrust of marketing campaigns.
- The priority of individual product development projects.
- The desirability of potential alliances.
- The capabilities to build into business processes.
- The structure of the organization.
- The performance that should be rewarded.

A strategy does not contain these decisions; it provides the backdrop for making these decisions. For example:

- A strategy that is based on growth through the development and introduction of new products drives different investments than one in which growth will result from selling existing products in new markets.
- Marketing plans are different in a business with a "few customers/deep penetration/lots of products" strategy than they are in a "limited range of products/as many customers as possible" strategy.
- Information technology needs are different in a company whose strategy has a business-to-business thrust than in a company with a business-to-consumer focus.
- A strategy based on winning through world-class customer service spawns different business process and human resource development than one in which the competitive advantage is low price. (Yes, you can enjoy both advantages.)
- An organization does not consider outsourcing manufacturing if its strategy has identified that competency as a key component of its competitive advantage.
- The processes and structure of a business that intends to generate 80 percent of its revenue through e-commerce is different from one in which the Internet is a vehicle for guiding people to its brick-and-mortar stores.

If "Why strategy?" had to be answered in one word, that word would be *focus*. If an organization had unlimited resources, it would not need a strategy. It could invest in anything that struck its executives' fancy. However, even ExxonMobil, Microsoft, and the government of Brunei have resource constraints, particularly when you consider the fact that money is not the only resource. One of an organization's most precious resources is the time and mindshare of its executives and managers.

In addition to guiding daily decision making and channeling the allocation of resources, a strategy:

- Establishes an organization's identity, which is critical to the market, current and potential employees, and the investment community.
- Creates the backbone of the culture.
- Defines high-level goals, from which all others should cascade.

Because strategy guides, channels, establishes, creates, and defines, it deserves the time it takes to debate it, document it, and deploy it.

■ DOES STRATEGY REQUIRE A STABLE BUSINESS ENVIRONMENT?

Some people believe that the pace of today's business environment makes strategy irrelevant. They see the constant changes in technology, customer expectations, the competitive landscape, and economic variables as rendering any strategy obsolete before it is bound and distributed. If so, why bother?

This point of view is based on a set of false assumptions:

- *Strategies take a long time to develop.* A robust, comprehensive strategy can rarely be hammered out in a one-day meeting. The strategy process requires collecting information and opinions, evaluating alternatives, and allowing time for ideas—particularly radical ideas—to germinate. Robust strategies go beyond "mission/vision/values" statements by documenting tough decisions regarding what is in and out of scope and the priorities of what is in. That takes time.

    However, that does not mean that strategy development has to be a yearlong exercise. Executives can develop a comprehensive, fact-based, compelling, specific strategy in a handful of days, scheduled over the span of two or three months. If a business is bleeding strategically, that time frame can be compressed.

■ *Strategies need to be in place, unchanged, for a long period of time.* Strategies used to be five- or ten-year visions. In sectors with long product development or regulatory approval cycles, those time frames are still appropriate. However, a strategic perspective can be as short as an industry requires it to be. The executives of a company in the turbulent computer network hardware industry have recently decided to develop their first long-term strategy. The time frame of this beyond-the-horizon vision? Twelve months.

Regardless of how far down the road they look, strategies should be dynamic. Triggers to examine a strategy, and change it if necessary, include:

➤ Goals are not being met.

➤ Strategic actions are not producing the expected reaction from the market, the competition, and/or the investment community.

➤ There is a major change in the external landscape (customers, competitors, technology, the economy, and the other factors described in Chapter 2).

➤ There is significant and well-founded internal resistance to implementing the strategy.

An executive team should review its strategy, and update it if necessary, at least once a year.

■ *Strategies should include price lists, marketing activities, department budgets, and information technology priorities.* If a strategy is cluttered with tactics, it legitimately can be seen as too temporary to be useful. For example, prices may need to be elastic to fit current supply-and-demand conditions. A strategy should not contain a price list; it should describe an organization's pricing philosophy (for example, "We will use our superior response time and post-sale service to justify a slight premium in price"). Pricing philosophy is not permanent, but its shelf life is long enough to justify articulation and codification in a strategy.

Marketing and sales tactics may need to change continuously to fit the season, the fickleness of the market, the actions of competitors, and raw material availability. However, a strategy should not contain marketing actions. It should describe the decisions that drive those actions: the company's positioning (for example, "We will be the premier provider of business hotel and conference services") and its competitive advantage (for example, "We will win based on our location, our flexibility, and our price-value equation"). Positioning and competitive advantage last long enough to merit debate in a strategy session and documentation in a strategy document.

- *Strategies are based on the personalities of the current leaders, who are not likely to be around for long.* Strategies carry the imprint of executives, particularly the CEO. Strategies do—and should—reflect a CEO's entrepreneurship, risk orientation, breadth of vision, experienced-based biases, and patience. However, the fact that executives tend to be transient is not an excuse for avoiding strategy. On the contrary, good strategies describe visions in a way that enables new chief executives to decide if and how they want them to change.

■ WHO SHOULD SET STRATEGY?

To many, strategy evokes the image of a group of planners, none of whom has ever met a customer, holed up in a corporate office tower crunching numbers and developing mind-numbing models and charts. While strategy formulation requires some staffwork, the vision should not come from staffers, consultants, or lower-level people who have been strategically empowered.

Strategy is the most important domain and, one could argue, the only domain, of the people who run the business. Strategy should be established—with input from others—by the CEO and his/her 4 to 12 top executives. They should not just bless it; they should create it. Their fingerprints should be on it. They should sweat over every decision and, in some sections, every word. As discussed in Chapter 3, strategy formulation is the primary responsibility of leaders.

While strategy implementation requires widespread partici-pation, executives should also lead that process.

■ WHAT IS THE APPROPRIATE LENGTH OF A STRATEGY DOCUMENT?

Many strategic documents are most valuable as doorstops. A strategy may be supported by solid research. It may wisely address each area listed under "What Questions Should a Strategy Answer?" It may be specific, motivating, and clearly worded. However, that is insufficient. Successful strategy deployment is dependent upon *accessibility*. The longer the strategic document, the greater the likelihood that those who need its guidance will not open it.

The best strategies contain three levels of detail:

- A 1- or 2-page strategic profile that contains the essence of the vision.
- An 8- to 12-page full strategy that contains the details of the product/market scope, emphasis, and mix.
- An as-many-pages-as-needed set of appendices that include the information and analysis supporting the assumptions and decisions.

Different audiences should get different levels of detail.

■ WHAT ARE TYPICAL STRATEGY WEAKNESSES?

The most common deficiencies in strategy formulation and implementation are:

- Not basing strategic decisions on a foundation of *self-under-standing* and *intelligence about the external environment,* espe-cially the market and the competition.
- Not basing the strategy on a *set of assumptions* about the future external environment.
- Overly focusing the strategy on the financials, rather than on *decisions regarding products, markets, and competitive advantage.*

- Failing to step up to the *tough strategic choices,* including what *not* to do (for example, services that will not be offered, markets that will not be served).

- Failing to consider *radical alternatives* before settling on a strategic direction.

- Mis-categorizing strengths (what an organization is good at) as *competitive advantages* (the small set of strengths that the market perceives as unique or superior).

- Limiting the strategy to mission, vision, and values statements that are not *specific enough* to drive daily decision making.

- Failing to develop a comprehensive, integrated, detailed, manageable *strategy implementation plan* that describes the changes necessary for the strategy to take root.

- Not providing the *human and financial resources* necessary to successfully implement the strategy in a reasonable amount of time.

- Not establishing a *hands-on executive role* in implementation.

- Failing to *project manage* implementation so that it remains under control and incorporates midcourse corrections when needed.

- Not hardwiring the strategy to *operational planning and budgeting.*

- Treating strategy formulation as a periodic, infrequent event rather than a *continuous process.*

➤ SELF-ASSESSMENT QUESTIONS

➤ *Do we have a business strategy? (If "no," ignore the questions that follow.)*

➤ *Do our people—at all levels—understand the role strategy should play in guiding daily activities?*

➤ *Is our strategy documented (as opposed to simply being in the CEO's head)?*

➤ *Is our strategy underpinned by a set of assumptions about the future external environment?*

➤ *Have we defined a strong, specific, measurable set of values/beliefs?*

> ➤ *Does our strategy define the markets we will and will not serve?*
> ➤ *Does our strategy define the needs we will and will not meet?*
> ➤ *Does our strategy define how we will win?*
> ➤ *Does our strategy identify the nature and amount of investment we will make in each product and market?*
> ➤ *Does our strategy identify the capabilities (process, skill, equipment, and facilities) we need to fulfill our vision?*
> ➤ *Have we developed strategic goals?*
> ➤ *Does our strategy reflect creative thinking?*
> ➤ *Did we seriously consider alternative strategies?*
> ➤ *Is our strategy compelling to its various constituencies (for example, customers, shareholders, employees)?*
> ➤ *Can our strategy be implemented in the real world?*
> ➤ *Do we have a comprehensive, manageable strategy implementation plan?*
> ➤ *Does our plan include projects that address both hard (for example,* goals *and* processes) *and soft (for example,* culture *and* leadership) *needs?*
> ➤ *Are we successfully implementing our plan?*
> ➤ *Do we monitor our strategic performance and review/ update our strategy periodically and when triggered by significant events?*

■ WHAT IS THE PROCESS FOR ADDRESSING THE STRATEGY VARIABLE?

You can address any "no" answers to the Self-Assessment Questions by ingraining a comprehensive strategy approach that embraces five phases (see Figure 4.2):

- In *Phase 1,* information on the external and internal business environments is collected and analyzed. The external environment includes the market, the competition, and the

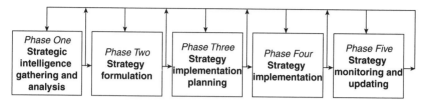

Figure 4.2 The Kepner-Tregoe Strategy Formulation and Implementation Process

other factors described in Chapter 2. The internal environment includes the current strategy, performance information, culture, employee perceptions, and product/market successes and failures. The output of Phase 1 is a set of assumptions about the future and a profile of the setting in which strategic decisions will be implemented. The assumptions and profile become the test bed for alternative strategies and the underpinning of the strategy that is selected.

Ken Weymouth, introduced at the beginning of this chapter, found that Health Aid had extensive market and competitive intelligence. However, some of this information was owned by Business Planning, some was commissioned by and housed in Marketing, some was in Sales, and the rest was in Research and Manufacturing. For the first time, he brought it all together.

Ken and his top team determined that their competitive intelligence was sufficiently complete and current to serve as a platform for the decisions they would be making in Phase 2. However, the market research, while useful, had gaping holes. It was strong in the pharmacy channel, weak in the department store channel, and nonexistent in the Internet channel. Other than by implication, it did not supplement customer information with consumer information; they had nothing but anecdotal information and guesses about their end users. It gave no insight into the medical equipment or international markets. Ken arranged for a market research study to fill in the gaps.

As the external research was being done, Ken commissioned an internal strategy audit. Based on a summary of multilevel interviews, surveys, key decision review, and document analysis, the executive team got a snapshot of Health Aid's de facto current strategy and employee perceptions of direction, capabilities, and vulnerabilities.

The executive team met to review the findings. Their assumptions about the future included:

➤ Consolidation of players in the pharmaceutical space would continue.

➤ The regulatory environment would be tougher domestically and unchanged internationally.

➤ Demand for prescription drugs would grow 5 to 7 percent per year. Medical equipment (everything from canes to pacemakers) would grow at 12 percent per year. Vitamins and other supplements would grow at 15 percent per year.

➤ Consumers would increasingly ask for generic drugs, would be more price conscious when purchasing over-the-counter medication, and would continue to migrate from stand-alone drug stores to discount department store pharmacies.

➤ Due to privacy concerns and minimal doctor involvement, there would be a backlash against the purchase of prescription drugs over the Internet. It would continue to be a significant force in the industry but was not going to render traditional channels obsolete.

■ In *Phase 2*, executives establish the strategic time frame (how far into the future to look), articulate their values/beliefs, and make the tough choices. These choices include products/services to offer and not offer, markets to serve and not serve, emphasis among products/services and markets, competitive advantage(s), capabilities, goals, and critical issues. The output of Phase 2 is the strategy.

The Health Aid top team made the following decisions during Phase 2:

➤ They decided that their vision would span the next three years.

➤ After wrenching soul-searching and some painful wordsmithing, they established eight value/belief statements. In terms of impact on their direction, the most dramatic one was "We will not offer any products that we can not differentiate through quality, packaging, or service."

➤ They would emphasize proprietary prescription drugs and branded over-the-counter medications. They would not get into the medical equipment business but would begin offering vitamins and proven herbal supplements. They would not private label.

➤ They would not abandon their traditional stand-alone pharmacy channel but would greatly increase their penetration of in-store pharmacies in major discount chains. They would not sell their supplements through health and nutrition outlets. They would closely monitor and respond to overtures from Internet-based direct-to-consumer health care companies. They would target educated consumers for whom brand is an important symbol of quality. They would explore alliances with companies in other countries with similar consumers and channels.

➤ They would win through the quality of their products; the attractiveness and user-friendliness of their packaging; their brand recognition; and their service to doctors, pharmacists, and consumers. While they would be price competitive, they would not strive to be the lowest-cost provider.

➤ Their key capabilities would include speedy product introduction, pharmacist and doctor relationship management, and consumer marketing.

➤ They would sustain 15 percent revenue growth and 20 percent profit growth during each of the next three years.

➤ They would supplement their existing metrics with those that measure consumer brand awareness and pharmacist relationship strength.

■ In *Phase 3,* executives identify the actions/projects/initiatives that will implement the strategy. Actions may need to be taken in any or all of these areas:

➤ New business entry/exit.

➤ Mergers and acquisitions.

➤ Product development.

> Market development.
> Business process (re)design.
> Information technology.
> Organization structure.
> Human competence development.

Phase 3 includes a game plan for communicating the strategy and cascading it through lower-level strategies. It includes the initiatives that will align the culture, policies, and measures with the strategy. Lastly, it contains the process by which the strategy will be monitored and kept current. Executives set priorities, analyze capacity, and determine the sequence of implementation projects. The output of Phase 3 is a Strategic Master Project Plan.

Health Aid's Strategic Master Project Plan included:

> Establishing substrategies in each division.
> Streamlining its product development and launch process.
> Improving sales force relationship management skills.
> Upgrading its Web site to reflect its new positioning.
> Installing a computer system that links it to the point-of-sale systems in its primary customers.
> Acquiring herbal supplement research capability, perhaps through acquisition.
> Establishing an alliance with a premier consumer marketing firm.
> Benchmarking firms in other industries that excel in postsale service and adopting their best practices.
> Exploring potential international alliances.
> Creating a service culture.

▪ In *Phase 4,* project managers at multiple levels carry out the initiatives planned in Phase 3, making midcourse corrections when necessary. This is the phase in which the dream becomes reality. This is the phase that requires the greatest investment of time and money. This is the phase that has buried many brilliant visions. Widespread involvement in Phase 4 is critical to building commitment, deploying the best internal and external technical expertise (for example, computer system design, job design, marketing program design), and dividing and conquering the tremendous amount of work.

In Phase 4, Health Aid carried out the ambitious plan it had created in Phase 3. Ken assigned a full-time strategy implementation manager to coordinate all of the projects. He set up a system for the ongoing monitoring of strategic performance. Strategy implementation became a standing agenda item in executive team meetings. The vice president of human resources oversaw the upgrade of project management skills among those with responsibility for strategy implementation initiatives.

- In *Phase 5*, the strategy is continuously monitored in terms of its viability (Is it working?), its underpinnings (Are the assumptions still valid?), and its implementation (Is it being carried out?). The top team conducts targeted and comprehensive strategy reviews and updates the strategy as needed.

Health Aid's executives vowed that they would not allow their strategy to become obsolete or be eclipsed by operational priorities. Their strategic monitoring system is designed to send up red flags when performance fails to meet expectations or Phase 1 assumptions are proved false. They have hardwired the strategy to the operational planning and budgeting system. They have established a strategy calendar that includes a biyearly, off-site two-day strategy review/update meeting.

To determine your organization's next steps:

- Use the Self-Assessment Questions to diagnose the current state of strategy in your organization.
- Enter the five-phase process at the point of your current need. You may not need to start at Phase 1. For example, your strategic intelligence and assumptions, while not perfect, may be an adequate foundation for the product/market decisions that you urgently need to make. In this situation, you can enter the process at Phase 2. Or your assessment

may show that your strategy is comprehensive, current, specific, and viable; your need is to plan for its implementation. If so, you would enter the process at Phase 3.

■ Take the formulation, planning, or implementation steps in the phase in which you have decided to start. Then, pursue the subsequent phases.

■ Develop a plan for ongoing strategy formulation and implementation.

In the Enterprise Model, *leadership* and *strategy* are the drivers. *Leadership* and *goals/measurement* are part of both strategy and strategy implementation. All of the other variables—*business processes, culture, human capabilities, information/knowledge management, organization structure/roles,* and *issue resolution*—are aspects of strategy implementation. As you will see in subsequent chapters, the assessment of each of these variables begins with a test of the degree to which your strategy provides the necessary guidance.

Chapter 5

Rethinking Business Processes

Jorge Sanchez is pleased with his new business strategy. As president of the Resort Division of Wethersfield Hotels, Inc., he is responsible for the 12 existing luxury resorts around the world and the new properties that are being added each year. While his division's performance has been solid for five years, his strategy is driven by his—and his CEO's—desire to greatly accelerate Wethersfield's growth in this hot market. In that strategy, he and his top team have:

- Altered the traditional definition of "resort."
- Expanded the categories of guests that will be targeted.
- Identified the areas in which Wethersfield will establish resorts.
- Decided to depart from Wethersfield's historic approach to expansion by pursuing the acquisition of existing properties in new markets rather than building new facilities.
- Clearly defined Wethersfield's competitive advantages in the resort space, which include the quality of its golf courses, entertainment, and recreational activities; the layout and service in its conference facilities; and its "no worries" service from airport pickup to airport drop-off.

While the strategic decision making was difficult, even contentious at times, it was exhilarating. The end game—the formulation of an aggressive growth vision—was always clear. However, Jorge is not looking forward to implementation of that strategy. He is not a "detail guy," but he does not think anyone else should assume

this key responsibility. The amount of work to be done is daunting. Worst of all, he does not know where to start.

Before he launches initiatives to address Wethersfield's structure, culture, skill development, and information systems needs, Jorge should put in place the business processes that will be the vehicles for his implementation journey.

As this is written, business processes have reclaimed their back-burner status. They had a prominent role in the quality movement, which in many organizations has become yesterday's news. Processes resurfaced, even took center stage, during the reengineering era. However, reengineering became a synonym for downsizing, costly and cumbersome information technology solutions, and operational tinkering that distracted executives from strategic decision making. As a result, the concept has fallen out of favor and, in many cases, the focus on business processes has died with it.

Some pundits argue that organizations have not lost sight of processes; they maintain that processes have become part of everyday consciousness and their continuous improvement has become ingrained. Unfortunately, that is true in only a select few organizations.

Contrarians celebrate the death of process design efforts, which they think dampened creativity, calcified operations that need to be flexible, and substituted procedure for talent. Processes *can* do that. In the wrong hands, so can business plans, budgets, computer systems, policies, and goals.

Well-designed processes actually stimulate creativity when it is desirable, build in flexibility where it is needed, and enable talented people to make their optimum contribution.

Love them or hate them, business processes are nothing less than the way work gets done. They may be complex or simple. They may be formally documented, jotted down on the back of an envelope, or they may reside in people's heads. They may be inflexible or constantly changing. They may be science or art. However, without processes, prospects cannot be turned into customers. An order does not result in a delivered service. New products fail to get developed and launched. People do not get hired or paid.

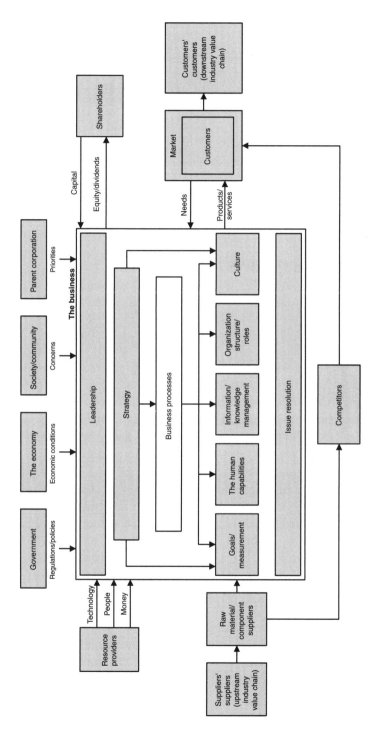

Figure 5.1 The Position of Business Processes in the Enterprise Model

Results are not produced by organization structures, by computer systems, by skills, or by cultures; they are produced by business processes. That is why they are at the epicenter of the Enterprise Model.

Processes are the organizational equivalent of automobile engines. They are not visible from the outside. They do not determine where you should go. To most people, they are not sexy. However, ignore the effectiveness and efficiency of your organization's workflows and you are likely to find yourself broken down by the side of the road.

■ WHAT ARE BUSINESS PROCESSES?

Business processes are the steps that convert inputs to outputs. For example, the process commonly called "order-to-cash" takes a customer order and ultimately converts it to money in the supplier's bank account. The conversion of an order to money generally includes subprocesses such as order entry, scheduling, product picking or manufacturing, packaging, shipping, invoicing, and collections. Each of these subprocesses has a series of steps that are carried out by people or machines.

The input to the order-to-cash process—a customer order—is the output of another process, typically called "business development." That process may start with a lead (a potential piece of business) and encompass the steps in closing a sale. Some organizations choose to define this process more broadly; they go upstream and identify the input as a target market/customer and include the marketing activities that result in leads. In some organizations, the business development process is different for different products, for different channels (for example, Internet versus face-to-face), or in different countries.

How do you make sure you have the right products? Through your market research and product development or product sourcing processes. How do you get the components or raw material that you need to configure your products? Through your purchasing and supplier management processes. How do you make sure you have products to sell? Through your forecasting, manufacturing, and inventory management processes.

How are customers' postsale needs met? Through your customer service and relationship management processes.

Similarly, you will be profitable only if you have well-oiled back-office processes (those that do not touch customers or suppliers directly) such as forecasting, budgeting, financial reporting, hiring, succession planning, and patent application.

You can outsource any of these line and staff processes, but they still remain your responsibility.

■ WHY ARE PROCESSES IMPORTANT?

One could argue that a business has only four dimensions:

- *Strategy* (which defines *what* work should be done).
- *Business processes* (which define *how* work should be done).
- *Issue resolution* (which defines how operational problems are solved, decisions are made, and opportunities are realized as the work is being done).
- *Leadership* (which sees that an energized workforce is pursuing the right strategy, carrying out intelligently designed processes, and efficiently resolving issues).

This breakdown is at a very high level. It is like saying that human health has only four dimensions: physical, mental, emotional, and spiritual. That statement may be accurate, but it is not specific enough to be actionable. If we do not make visible and examine enabling variables such as culture, human competencies, and structure, we are unlikely to identify and meet needs in those areas.

While this "only four variables" view is too simplistic to thoroughly diagnose and improve organization health, it does give processes the prominence they deserve. For example:

- You can have visionary *leadership,* but if the business processes do not work, the leader does not have vehicles for implementing the vision.
- You can have an enlightened *culture* (for example, one characterized by appropriate treatment of customers and employees, participation in decision making, risk orientation, and

emphasis on innovation), but that culture cannot compensate for ineffective or inefficient processes.

- You can have world-class talent (*human capabilities*), but poorly defined processes will hold people back from their maximum contribution, de-motivate them, and ultimately cause the best of them to leave.
- You can have state-of-the-art *information systems*, but they are only as good as the business processes they support.
- You can have balanced, challenging organizationwide *goals*, but if they are not translated into process goals, these targets remain on the mountaintop, unconnected to the levers that determine whether they are hit.
- You can have an *organization structure* with distinct department missions, clear reporting relationships, and ample budgets. However, work is not accomplished by the structure, but by the processes that flow through the structure.

■ WHAT SHOULD DRIVE PROCESSES?

As the Enterprise Model depicts, strategy, with leadership behind it, should drive processes. A review of your strategy should enable you to determine:

- *The processes that should be in place.* Does successful deployment of your strategy require a merger/acquisition process? a market entry process? a technical support process? a supplier management process? a market research process?
- *The priority of processes.* Based on the amount of your growth that will come from new products, what is the priority of your product development process? Based on the human capabilities you need and the supply of those skills in the job market, what is the priority of your recruiting/hiring process? Based on your funding requirements, what is the priority of your cash management process?
- *The capabilities of processes.* If you have identified response time as a competitive advantage, have you built speed into your customer inquiry process? If you have identified product customization as a competitive advantage, have you built flexibility into your manufacturing process? If you

have identified real-time market-demand knowledge as a competitive advantage, have you built point-of-sale customer information collection into your production scheduling and inventory management processes?

■ WHAT SHOULD PROCESSES DRIVE?

Processes, with the guiding hands of strategy and leadership behind them, should drive all of the variables that appear below them in the Enterprise Model. Specifically:

- *Goals/measurement* (see Chapter 6). Enterprisewide goals are part of the strategy. Processes are the bridges between strategic goals and targets for the men and women doing the work. For example, your strategy probably contains metrics for revenue, net income, and return on assets. Departments, teams, and individuals do not understand how they can contribute to these financial results until they have been translated into metrics at the end of and upstream in processes such as business development, order fulfillment, and product development.
- *Culture* (see Chapter 7). Culture is the norms of behavior. It includes actions you can see and hear (for example, the way you interact with customers and run meetings), the nature and enforcement of policies and practices (for example, levels of budget authority and the performance that is rewarded), and intangible relationship factors (for example, power and trust). Because it is deeply rooted, culture in a mature organization is difficult and time consuming to change. However, culture should be the servant—not the master—of strategy and processes. For example, airline executives need to create a culture that supports the decision-making authority they want ticket agents to exercise during the check-in process.
- *Human capabilities* (see Chapter 8). Processes, with the exception of the few that are entirely automated, are sets of tasks carried out by people. Process outputs and activities should define the physical and mental skills, the knowledge, and the emotional makeup that people need to perform

those tasks. For example, an in-store sales process requires floor personnel to have product knowledge, communication skills, customer relationship skills, cash register/credit card skills, and the ability to multitask in a high-pressure environment.

- *Information/knowledge management* (see Chapter 9). One of the common deficiencies in the installation of enterprise resource planning systems is that processes are designed to meet the needs of the computer system rather than vice versa. The questions, in sequence, should be:

    1. What are the *outputs* we expect from this process?
    2. What are the *steps* through which we will produce these outputs?
    3. What do we want to *learn* from our successes and failures in this process?
    4. In what ways can *information technology* enable us to more effectively and efficiently carry out those steps and learn from our experience?

    For example, only after you have designed your optimum financial planning and reporting process are you in a position to determine the software that will best support it.

- *Structure/roles* (see Chapter 10). Departments are purely resource groupings that are necessary for administrative purposes. While organization structure design—the drawing of departmental boundaries, the development of department missions, and the identification of who will be in each department—is an important performance variable, it should be subordinate to business processes. Again, work gets done through processes.

    When presented with evidence that your customer complaint resolution process does not work, "Yes, but we have role clarity and appropriate spans of control" is not a very compelling response.

- *Issue resolution* (see Chapter 11). Quality and speed of issue resolution are a function of four factors:

1. The accuracy, completeness, and accessibility of *information.*
2. The viability and utility of any institutionalized *methods* for issue resolution (for example, the published protocol for troubleshooting equipment failures and the template to be used when selecting an employee for a job).
3. The nature and extent of *participation.*
4. Individual and team problem-solving, problem-avoidance, decision-making, and project-management *skills.*

Business processes ought to drive all four of these factors. For example, the purchasing process should guide the generation and storage of purchasing information, the creation of purchasing-decision templates, the identification of the people who should participate in purchasing decisions, and the development of the skills that should be in the repertoire of those who contribute to purchasing decisions.

■ WHAT ARE TYPICAL PROCESS WEAKNESSES?

The most significant process deficiency is not having one.

- If a process has not been designed and communicated, people engage in activities that are not coordinated, compromising quality and efficiency. ("You do that? So do I.")
- If you have to start with a clean piece of paper every time you do something like developing a product or a business plan, you waste time and energy. ("Now, where should we begin?")
- Without processes, you lack mechanisms for institutionalizing the learning from previous journeys down the same trail. ("I seem to remember that we tried that before and it failed.")
- Working in an environment without a common process is a frustrating experience. ("If we are all supposed to be serving the same customer, why are we not all on the same page?")

- Without a process, an organization relies on individual hero-ics that, while noble, hardly form the basis of a world-class operation. ("I do not feel like slaying any dragons today.")

If a process exists, it may have one or more of three types of deficiency: design, execution, and management.

A process *design* is suboptimal if it has:

- *Weak connections across functional lines.* The sales and man-ufacturing steps in a new product development process may work well, but the process will suffer if the interface between the sales and manufacturing departments is non-existent or clumsy.
- *Bottlenecks.* All inbound and outbound logistics may have to flow through plant scheduling, which is swamped with work. As a result, the organization experiences delays in getting materials in and sending products out.
- *Non-value-added steps.* A forecasting process may include a review meeting that does nothing to improve the quality of the forecasts and drains time from valuable resources. The information that is exchanged in these meetings could be made available electronically.
- *Steps carried out in series that should be in parallel.* A market-ing literature development process may require all brochures to be run by legal before being sent to sales for critique. These reviews could be concurrent.
- *Steps carried out by the wrong people.* An order fulfillment process may require order information to be gathered by inside sales, which forwards it to finance for coding and entering into the system. The quality, cycle time, and cost of this subprocess would be improved if inside sales entered orders.
- *Steps done manually or with ineffective computer support.* A distribution process may require the manipulation of three separate databases that do not talk to one another, resulting in increased cycle time and diminished job satisfaction.
- *Too many or too few controls.* A product development process can be designed so tightly that there is no room for creativ-ity or no mechanism for funding the off-the-wall ideas that may revolutionize the industry and fuel a company's

growth. Or the process can be so loose that it allows almost any idea to achieve official project status and to be pursued long after it has become clear that it is off strategy or will never succeed in the marketplace. This absence of controls (go/no-go gates in the process) increases cost and decreases focus on high-potential opportunities.

A process may be well designed. In other words, the boxes and arrows in the flow diagram make sense. However, that process may be ineffective or inefficient due to what does or does not happen *within* the boxes. The *execution* of a process is deficient if:

- *It lacks sufficient resources.* An organization's executives may have decided that growth will be fueled primarily by new products; however, only half of one person is dedicated to the critical market research step in the product development process, and she is on maternity leave. Or people in a financial reporting process may not have access to a piece of software that facilitates the consolidation and display of information.
- *People do not have the necessary skills.* A business development process suffers if sales representatives are good at pitching a product but lack the ability to identify customer needs. A computer troubleshooting process is not effective if help desk personnel cannot communicate with users in terms they understand.
- *The reward system does not encourage desired behaviors.* A software installation process may include steps in which technicians are expected to identify additional business opportunities and communicate them to sales. However, they are measured and rewarded for accurate and speedy installation, not the quality or quantity of the business opportunities they unearth. As a result, they do not invest time in this activity. Either the incentives should change or the technicians should be taken out of the lead-generation business.

A process may be well designed. It may not have resource, skill, or incentive deficiencies. However, if it is not well managed,

design and execution deficiencies are likely to remain undetected. Process *management* shortcomings include:

- *No ownership.* Intrafunctional processes, like insurance
  claim processing or vehicle maintenance, are the responsibility of the person who heads that function and therefore
  part of normal managerial oversight. However, who owns
  cross-functional processes like new product development?
  Is it Research and Development? Marketing? Sales? Most
  often, the answer is "nobody." Without a focal owner, each
  function optimizes its part of the process, often resulting in
  the suboptimization of the whole.
- *Nonexistent or ineffective measurement.* As discussed in Chapter 6, measurement is a tool for comparing performance to
  expectations. An organization that is not measuring its
  processes is not measuring the way work gets done. If your
  company only measures end-of-process performance (for
  example, delivery cycle time and safety incidents), you take
  action based solely on what economists call "lagging indicators." These after-the-fact measures should be supplemented by "leading indicators" (for example, order entry
  time and conformance to safety policies). Upstream metrics
  enable you to avoid problems or resolve them before they
  become serious.
- *No strategy-driven process plans.* If processes are to play the
  central role described previously and depicted in the Enterprise Model, they need to be a pivotal part of planning. If
  your strategy is deployed solely through the boxes on the
  organization chart, you are subordinating the role of the
  cross-functional processes that are the heart of the way
  work gets done. The quality of cross-functional processes is
  determined as much by what goes on *between* the boxes
  (the white space on the organization chart[1]) as *within* the
  boxes. Once the strategy has been formulated and you are
  ready to deploy it through operational plans and budgets,
  you should be asking: "What is our product development
  plan?" "What is our supply chain plan?" "What is our customer service plan?"

➤ SELF-ASSESSMENT QUESTIONS

➤ *Have we identified our core (strategically most important) and noncore business processes?*

➤ *Have we documented our processes?*

➤ *Have we identified and eliminated the process design deficiencies listed above?*

➤ *Have we identified and eliminated the process execution deficiencies listed above?*

➤ *Have we ensured that cross-functional processes have owners?*

➤ *Do we measure process outputs and upstream process performance?*

➤ *Is process effectiveness/efficiency the basis of our organization structure decisions?*

➤ *Is process effectiveness/efficiency the basis of our information system decisions?*

➤ *Do individuals/teams have the skills and the charter to resolve process issues?*

➤ *Does our culture support optimum process performance?*

■ WHAT IS THE PROCESS FOR PROCESS (RE)DESIGN?

The process for designing or redesigning a business process is:

1. *Identify the process(es) to be improved.* Based on an examination (and upgrade, if necessary) of the business strategy, your executive team identifies the organization's highest-priority processes. These include processes that provide competitive advantages, as well as those that require significant investment to maintain or be brought to competitive parity. The team then identifies the needs for each of these priority processes—creation, radical redesign, incremental improvement, or ongoing management—and develops a plan to meet those needs.

Wethersfield Hotels' Jorge Sanchez, introduced at the beginning of this chapter, met with his top team to develop the implementation plan for their new strategy. They concluded that any decisions regarding organization structure, information technology, measurement systems, and culture should follow the identification and scrutiny of the Resort Division's business processes.

While all of the division's processes could have benefitted from analysis and improvement, the executives realized that they could not tackle everything at once. They decided to focus initially on those processes that were most critical to strategic success. After examining their target markets, core services, and competitive advantages, they identified their core processes and requirements to be:

➤ The acquisitions process. They defined this process as including acquisition candidate identification, due diligence, nonlegal/financial evaluation, and assimilation. Since no protocols for acquisitions existed internally, they quickly realized that this process needed to be *created*.

➤ The market research process. This process was a high priority because the strategy involved entering new markets, and Wethersfield was not strong in market intelligence gathering. They determined that this process needed *radical redesign*.

➤ The end-to-end customer service process. They defined customer service as including transportation; baggage handling; currency exchange; and concierge, check-in/out, and room service. To keep this umbrella process manageable, they excluded housekeeping and the processes associated with the restaurants, golf course, conference center, and recreation center. Since customer service is a current strength, they decided that this process needed *incremental improvement*.

They developed a plan for meeting the needs in each of these three areas. This core process plan was dovetailed with the strategy implementation actions that needed to go on in parallel and those that needed to follow it.

2. *Structure a process improvement project.* For each process that needs to be created, redesigned, or improved, the executive team identifies a process owner and a management oversight body (the "guidance team") that (1) sets project goals, (2) identifies project boundaries, and (3) designates the "process design team" that will conduct the process analysis and blueprint.

    Jorge assigned a subset of the Resorts Division top team as the guidance team for the creation of an acquisitions process. The vice president of corporate development was assigned as the process owner. They established *process goals* that included:

    ➤ By the end of next year, one acquisition completed and two in the pipeline.

    ➤ No smoking guns discovered after closing.

    ➤ Within nine months after the closing, initial acquisition totally integrated into Wethersfield operations.

    ➤ A due diligence/evaluation subprocess that takes ≤ 90 days, even for a complex deal.

    They established *project goals* that included:

    ➤ Process defined by the end of the year.

    ➤ Process to incorporate merger and acquisition best practices.

    ➤ Process to outsource activities that are not among Wethersfield's core competencies.

    The guidance team determined that the selection of geographic areas for resorts, the development of acquisition candidate criteria, and the ongoing management of newly acquired resorts were beyond the scope of this project. They designated a process design team that included representatives from Finance, Legal, Marketing, and Operations.

3. *Document and analyze the current process.* If, as is typically the case, a process (or at least a set of activities) already exists, the process design team documents it and identifies its strengths and weaknesses. Analyzing the current process builds understanding across the

entire team, highlights areas that need to be changed and those that are working well, and establishes the starting point for the implementation plan that will be developed in Step 6.

Since the Resorts Division had only made one small acquisition, there was not an institutionalized process to analyze. For that reason, the executive team described the need for this process as "create" rather than "improve." The process design team examined the steps that were followed in the one acquisition that had been made, interviewed the participants and sponsors, and documented what went well and did not go well. These lessons learned became one of the inputs to Step 4.

4. *Design the future process.* In this step, the process design team members embark on the creative part of the project. Using the project goals from Step 2, customer requirements and desires, the strengths and weaknesses identified in Step 3, team members' knowledge and experience, benchmarking information, a challenging facilitator, and input from others not on the team, they envision a number of alternative future processes. They then use a set of rigorously developed criteria to evaluate the options. They often end up creating a hybrid that incorporates the strengths of several alternatives. The goal is not merely improvement; it is to construct a first-class process that meets the goals established in Step 2.

Because the guidance team wanted the acquisition process to incorporate best practices, the process design team formally benchmarked four companies that were generally recognized as "best of breed" in acquisitions. They did extensive library research on other acquisition successes and failures and read the books written by the merger and acquisition gurus. They examined the Wethersfield corporate acquisitions process. This benchmarking information, the lessons learned from Step 3, and the directions from the guidance team became the primary stimuli for their generation of three alternative processes. One of these processes was lean; one was much more comprehensive in nonlegal/ financial areas such as culture; and the third represented a

middle ground. They were careful to not prematurely discuss who should carry out each step in the process.

They then used the Decision Analysis process described in Chapter 11 to evaluate the relative strengths of these alternatives. Their 15 selection criteria included:

➤ Identify dealbreakers as early as possible.

➤ Minimize the likelihood that an acquired company will not be able to be fully integrated within 24 months.

➤ Minimize time-to-close.

As a result of this analysis, they selected the more comprehensive process. Because this process did not fare well against the time objective, they redesigned it to have more activities occur in parallel. After they reached consensus on the steps in the future process, they identified the organizations that should carry out each step. Consistent with the guidelines they had been given, they recommended that quite a few of the activities be outsourced.

The process design team presented the recommended process to the guidance team, who approved it with two small changes. Their approval was limited to the concept of and the steps in the process; the executives would not commit to taking any action until they better understood the steps and cost of implementation (Step 6).

5. *Develop process metrics/goals.* As discussed in Chapter 6, process goals link strategic goals to department and team/individual goals. The team establishes both end-of-process (lagging) indicators as well as upstream (leading) indicators. These measures, which enable the process to be continuously monitored and improved, include both customer-focused dimensions like quality and cycle time and internal factors like cost and safety.

Armed with the tentative approval of the acquisitions process, the process design team developed a set of recommended end-of-process metrics. They included:

➤ Financial targets.

➤ Percentage of key people who remain after the acquisition.

> Cycle time from candidate identification to assimilation. (To make sure that there was no misinterpretation of this metric, they developed a comprehensive definition of "assimilation.")

After getting the guidance team's approval of these metrics, they developed a set of upstream (leading) indicators. For example, they inserted a time metric after the letter of intent, due diligence, deal closing, and rebranding subprocesses.

6. *Develop the implementation plan.* During this step, the team, with extensive input from others, creates a comprehensive plan for implementing the new process. This plan includes not only changes to the process flow but also any changes that need to be made in policies, resources, information systems, forms, job designs, skills, and reward systems. Regardless of the nature and extent of change, the plan for communicating the "what, why, and how" to all stakeholders is a key output. A process for plan development is provided in Chapter 11.

   The Wethersfield process design team created a high-level list of steps that had to be taken to implement the acquisitions process. Next to each step, they recorded the maximum cost and time. Since there was not an old process to undo, they focused on the new steps and roles. After the guidance team approved their work at this level, a broader group was assigned to develop the more detailed plan.

7. *Implement the plan.* In this step, participation increases well beyond what it has been in previous phases of the project. Widespread involvement ensures that (1) implementation will be accomplished in an acceptable amount of time; (2) technical experts in areas like systems design and job design are leading those aspects of implementation; and (3) the commitment critical to the success of the new process is generated throughout the organization.

   In this step, the Resorts Division acquisition team carried out the process installation plan developed in Step 6.

While some steps were taken immediately (for example, identifying the external legal and audit firms that would handle most of the due diligence), the executives did not want to do too much in a vacuum. Most steps in the process would be implemented in real time, as the first acquisition candidates were identified.

8. *Manage the process.* The process owner and guidance team determine how the new process will be managed and continuously improved. Process management activities typically include establishing process plans and budgets, building a measurement system around the process metrics, and conducting regular process reviews.

The guidance team affirmed the selection of the vice president of corporate development as the process owner. They designated a permanent cross-functional process management team. They created a system for regular top team reviews of performance against the metrics. The owner prepared a three-year process plan and budget that double-clicked on the acquisition targets in the strategy. The process management team blocked out two days on their calendar for a six-month review of the effectiveness and efficiency of the process.

Your first step is to diagnose your organization's business process health by asking the Self-Assessment Questions. Then, you will be prepared to enter the eight-step process at the point that addresses your need. For example, you may have to refine your strategy before any business process work is initiated. Or you may have already identified your strategic processes and the action they require (Step 1). Some of your strategic processes may need to be redesigned via Steps 2 through 7. Others, because they have a well-documented and analyzed current process, can begin with Step 4. Others may be healthy enough to go right to Step 8.

Based on the starting points for each core process, develop a creation/improvement/management plan that establishes the priority, sequence, ownership, and high-level resources for all of your process efforts. Regardless of where you begin with each individual process, your plan should include Step 8: designing an infrastructure and set of practices for the ongoing improvement and management of your processes.

With *leadership, strategy,* and *business processes* as the supporting pylons, we can address each of the remaining components in the Enterprise Model. As we explore each variable, we will answer a central question: How can we best support the way work gets done, which is through business processes?

■ NOTE

1. Geary Rummler and Alan Brache, *Improving Performance: How to Manage the White Space on the Organization Chart* (San Francisco: Jossey-Bass. 1995).

Chapter 6

Setting Goals and Measuring Progress

Ellen Robbins wishes that the corporate Performance Enhancement (PE) staff would just go away. Unfortunately, because these internal consultants have the ear of senior management, they cannot be ignored. As a district manager overseeing 15 Fill Your Tank convenience stores, she has more pressing concerns than dealing with their latest crusade, which is installing a measurement system.

Intuitively, she can not argue with the PE staffers' mantras of "What gets measured gets done" and "If it is not being measured, it is not being managed." However, her 22 years in retail have soured her on measurement.

- She thinks that organizations measure what is easy to measure rather than what is really important. Anything other than financial indicators always seem to be either off-the-mark or surrogates for true success.
- She has never worked in or around a measurement system that could not be beaten. She has seen too many managers twist or even fabricate the facts to make the numbers come out the way they should. Or, if the measurement books cannot be cooked, managers spend their time concocting elaborate "the dog ate my homework" explanations. In her more cynical moments, she wonders whether measurement is really a management ploy to stimulate creativity.
- She has been in environments that encourage people to work to the metrics the same way some educators teach to the test.

When goals are achieved, it is often at the expense of other factors that are at least as important.
- All too often, she has seen measurement used as a club. Like her father's belt and her parochial school teacher's ruler (the dreaded "knuckle whacker"), they are to be avoided at all cost. Because they are vehicles for punishment, any constructive purpose is lost.
- Her biggest beef concerns the cost-benefit equation. Even when goals play a legitimate role, she thinks their contribution is far outweighed by the time consumed by information collection, documentation, and reporting. Computers lighten the load somewhat, but the return still does not justify the investment.

Ellen is a good soldier who will comply with whatever program the performance enhancement people develop. However, she hopes that this campaign consumes a minimal amount of time and inflicts a manageable amount of pain.

Management fads come and go. However, measurement has been an ingredient in every prominent performance improvement recipe during the last 40 years. Management by Objectives, the rage of the late 1960s and 1970s, was a goal-based system. The dominant movement of the 1980s was Total Quality Management. All of the quality gurus (including those who, like W. Edwards Deming, had concerns about goals) preached measurement. The most widely used quality methods, generically called "statistical process control," had a central measurement component.

The 1990s brought us reengineering, cycle time management, activity-based costing, shareholder value, and the balanced scorecard, all of which were measurement-based systems. As this is written in 2001, the most popular operational improvement crusade is a born-again program of the early 1990s, Six Sigma, which has measurement at its core.

We should not be surprised that measurement is a theme that runs through high-impact improvement approaches. It enables an organization to keep score. It is—or should be—the basis for management decision making. However, it keeps surfacing in different guises because of the pervasiveness of reactions like Ellen's.

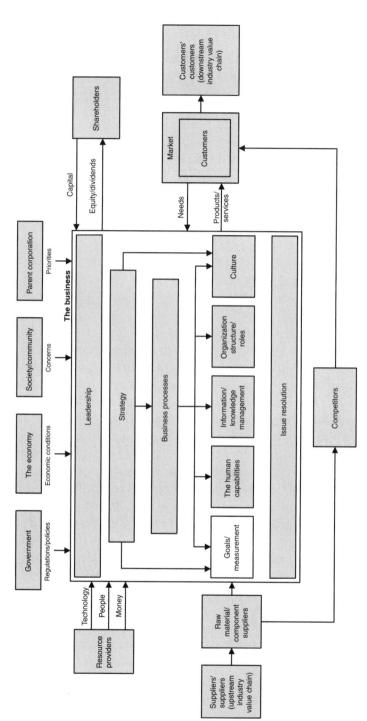

Figure 6.1 The Position of Goals/Measurement in the Enterprise Model

■ WHAT ARE GOALS AND WHERE DO THEY COME FROM?

Goals are objectives, targets, expectations. They are not unattainable dreams. They should not reflect what you have done, what others have done, or even what you could do. They should reflect what your customers need, what other constituencies in your external environment (see Chapter 2) need, and what your business needs to thrive.

Your business strategy (see Chapter 4) should include key indicators of strategic success that enable you to answer two questions:

- Are we implementing our strategy?
- Is that strategy working?

For example, in addition to financial measures, you may want to track your strategic performance through metrics such as customer satisfaction ratings, market share, percentage of sales from target products, average order size, and percentage of repeat business. In areas of scarce, mission-critical talent, "percentage of job offers that are accepted" may qualify as a strategic measure.

Your strategic indicators and decisions should be specific enough to enable you to identify your highest-priority external and internal operational-level "business drivers." For example, your strategy identifies a target market, the ante for playing in that market, and how you are going to beat your competition in that market. Customers in that market may require that products be installed and operational within a certain amount of time. They demand a certain level of quality. They require certain levels of service. They will not pay more than a certain price.

People who live near your facilities demand clean air and water and an attractive property. Your shareholders require stock appreciation and uninterrupted dividends. Internally, you need to keep cost below a certain level. Your employees have to conform to policies. You must have a safe work environment. You will succeed only if you maintain a stable workforce.

These drivers become the areas in which you should establish organizationwide goals, which become the basis for goals at lower levels.

Goals are only half of the equation. Even strategy-driven, specific, and balanced goals are worthless without the measurement systems that track performance against those goals, feed the performance information to the right people, and equip those people to make intelligent use of the information.

Measures answer the question "As evidenced by what?" For example, the success of your strategy may depend on a high level of brand awareness. As evidenced by what?

Once the unit of measurement has been determined, a goal answers the question "Compared to what?" Perhaps you have decided to measure brand awareness by the percentage of market research survey respondents who accurately recognize your brand. After conducting that survey, you know that your brand awareness is 76%. Compared to what?

■ WHY BOTHER WITH GOALS?

Appropriate goals and effective, efficient measurement systems ensure that you do not lose sight of your highest-priority external and internal needs. Furthermore, they help make certain that these needs dictate your decision-making agenda. Goals enable you to:

- Calibrate your expectations. For example, an executive team may quickly agree with this statement: "We will win in the automotive market through our exemplary customer service." However, this noble aim becomes a universally understood, deployable commitment only after the executives agree on how customer service will be assessed (the measure) and the level of service to which they aspire (the goal).
- Determine whether your strategy is on track.
- Translate your strategy into operations.
- Ensure that everyone's contribution is linked to the strategy.
- Monitor and evaluate day-to-day operations.
- Clearly communicate priorities.
- Identify problems that need to be solved.

- Specifically convey the results expected from processes, departments, teams, and individuals.
- Provide pinpointed feedback.
- Establish a clear and fact-based foundation for rewards.

Installing a goal/measurement system is hard work. However, this list of benefits shows that the return justifies the investment.

■ AT WHAT LEVELS SHOULD GOALS BE ESTABLISHED?

Goals and monitoring/feedback systems should be established at five levels:

1. *Strategic goals.* As we discussed in Chapter 4, one of the outputs of strategy formulation is a set of goals that will tell you whether you are on the right path. Should you measure revenue and profit growth? shareholder value? market share? customer retention rate? product prices vis-à-vis competitors' prices? volume of business from outside the country? percentage of revenue from new products? Having determined the metrics that are most meaningful, you can establish the target for each.

2. *Businesswide operational goals.* These goals are not strategic but are indicators of the overall health of your business. Should you measure revenue per professional? days without a recordable safety incident? employee retention rate? number of days' sales outstanding? (For some companies, the metrics in these examples may be strategic, not operational; for others, they may be process-specific, not businesswide.)

3. *Process goals.* At this, the most frequently overlooked of the five levels, end-of-the-line and upstream goals tell you whether your business processes (for example, business development, product development, order fulfillment) are making the necessary contribution to the business strategy. Should you measure proposal win

rate? number of products at various places in the development pipeline? average order-to-receipt cycle time? value of warranty claims?

4. *Departmental goals.* Most core business processes are cross functional. After you understand what constitutes success for those processes, you can identify the metrics and goals for the departments that contribute to those processes. For example, one of your measures for the cross-functional order-to-cash process may be "promise dates met." Based on that, you can establish cycle time goals for departments such as Inside Sales, Manufacturing, Distribution, and Finance. Similarly, you can establish quality and cost goals for each department based on the overall process goals in these areas.

5. *Team/individual goals.* Once your departmental goals are clear, you can develop the goals for the teams and individuals that work in those departments. Your Distribution Department's goals may include: "100 percent of orders accurate and complete"; "72 hours from 'pick order' to customer receipt of product;" and "Distribution cost average < $600/order." People within Distribution would have goals for product picking accuracy and cycle time, product breakage (which reflects on packaging quality and cost), address accuracy, packaging materials waste, on-time deliveries, and average shipping cost per order.

■ WHAT ARE TYPICAL WEAKNESSES IN GOAL SETTING AND MEASUREMENT?

Common deficiencies in goal setting/measurement include:

- *Failing to identify all of the important performance dimensions.* Perhaps you should measure not just revenue but also customer satisfaction; not just throughput but also variation; not just product development cycle time but the number of concepts in the "ideation" phase; not just sales per salesperson but also salesperson retention. A "balanced score-card"[1] ensures that you measure all relevant aspects of per-for-mance and give each the weight it deserves.

- *Establishing ambiguous (that is, open-to-interpretation) measures.* "95 percent customer satisfaction" is specific, but begs the "As evidenced by what?" question. Should we measure the amount of repeat business? customer retention rate? number of complaints? percentage of "Excellent/Good" responses on a customer satisfaction survey?
- *Developing impractical measures.* A hotel chain measure such as "Percentage of guests who work for Fortune 500 companies, stay with us over 10 nights per year, and were referred to us by their business colleagues" might surface illuminating information. However, tracking performance against this measure may require a bureaucracy that would bring the organization to its knees.
- *Focusing solely on "lagging indicators."* By the time you get a profit-and-loss statement, a safety incident report, or the results of a customer satisfaction survey, the horse is out of the barn. This after-the-fact information is essential, but should be supplemented by leading indicators that tell you how you are doing—and trigger action if necessary—well in advance.
- *Failing to benchmark,* within and outside your industry, to discover what performance levels are possible.
- *Focusing only internally.* You need to measure productivity, quality, cost, safety, and employee retention. However, do you also monitor how the economy is performing? the progress of regulatory legislation that could affect you? the buying trends in your target markets? your competitors' strategic and tactical moves? During your strategy deliberations (see Chapter 4), you should have made an assumption in each of these areas. Measurement enables you to determine whether your assumptions are proving to be true.
- *Failing to link measures* to the measures that feed them. For example, you probably measure sales volume. Do you know, and measure, the variables that influence that metric (perhaps dollar volume of proposals outstanding, average project size, and percentage of new customers)? Then, do

you measure the factors that influence each of these variables? (For example, your percentage of new customers may be a function of the number of marketing mailings and the close rate.) Do you cascade your measures to the point at which they continue to add value without creating a measurement bureaucracy?

- *Measuring activities rather than results.* Number of sales calls per week, number of people trained per year, and number of minutes per customer transaction are precise and trackable metrics, but are they capturing what is important?

- *Measuring everything that moves.* Anything *can* be measured. That does not mean that everything *should* be measured. With an excessive number of dials on the instrument panel (usually more than eight for any one organization, process, team, or individual), (1) too much time that could be spent performing is devoted to measuring performance and (2) the critical few metrics can be lost amidst the noise of other measurement.

- *Basing goals on fantasy, history, or assumed capability* rather than on the external and/or internal business need. If your customers will only do business with vendors that can fill an order in 24 hours, if your parent corporation requires 20 percent revenue growth, or if you can only make money with 95 percent uptime, it does not matter what others are doing or what you have done in the past.

- *Failing to develop an ongoing, easy-to-use measurement system.* A set of goals without a measurement system is like playing to win but not keeping score. With a deficient measurement system, you may be keeping score but withholding critical information from the coaches and players. If you communicate the score only once every 30 minutes, key people lack the information they need to steer the team to victory. If you provide your point total without comparing it to the other team's, the information is meaningless.

- *Lacking the discipline* to use the measurement system. Measuring and feeding back results can be time intensive. It is nobody's idea of a good time. However, measurement is the backbone of performance management. As with nearly everything else in management, the return is based on the investment.

➤ SELF-ASSESSMENT QUESTIONS

➤ Do we have a comprehensive, appropriate set of goals that describe strategic success?

➤ Do we have appropriate goals for each factor in our external environment (customers, suppliers, resource providers, competitors, shareholders, and other outside influences)?

➤ Do we have a comprehensive, appropriate set of goals for our overall internal business operations (quality, cost, time, safety)?

➤ Do we have a comprehensive, appropriate set of goals at the end of each of our business processes?

➤ Does each process have upstream (early warning) goals?

➤ Does each department have a comprehensive, appropriate set of goals?

➤ Do teams and individuals have a comprehensive, appropriate set of goals?

➤ Are strategic and operational business goals linked to process goals, department goals, and team/individual goals?

➤ Do we revise our goals to reflect new realities?

➤ Do we have a measurement system that efficiently and accurately captures how we are doing in terms of our goals?

➤ Do we use our measurement system to its full potential?

➤ Does our measurement system provide a solid return on its investment?

■ WHAT IS THE PROCESS FOR DEVELOPING GOALS AND MEASUREMENT SYSTEMS?

At each of the five levels—strategy, companywide operations, business processes, departments, and teams/individuals—the goal/measurement process has four steps. Table 6.1 displays these steps, with two examples of each.

Table 6.1 The Steps in the Measurement Process

Measurement Development Step	Word Processing Example	Business Development Example
1. Identify the performance dimensions that are important to measure (volume? quality? cycle time? cost? safety?).	Presentation materials quality	Depth of customer relationships
2. Select the most informative units of measurement.	Number of errors per presentation	Three-year rolling average annual sales volume per customer
3. Determine the goal for each measure.	No errors	$200,000 of sales per customer per year for three years
4. Develop a measurement system that tracks actual performance.	Feedback from presenters to word processors within 24 hours of presentation	Automated report generated as part of the weekly sales tracking system

Step 4 is the greatest challenge. There are far more examples of organizations with great metrics that are being underutilized than there are examples of great measurement systems that are tracking performance against lousy metrics. Once the measures and goals have been established (Steps 1 through 3 above), you need a measurement system that answers these questions:

- How will we *measure* our actual performance? (Will it be automated or manual? Who will take responsibility for information collection? Will the information be analyzed before it is distributed?)
- How *frequently* will the information be captured and disseminated?
- How will the performance information be *displayed* (a matrix? a pie chart? a graph with a trend line?)?
- Who will *receive* the information?
- What *actions* are the recipients expected to take based on the information?
- Who is responsible for identifying, finding the cause of, and eliminating the *gaps* between actual performance and the goals?

- How will we make sure that measurement information is used as the basis for *decision making?*
- How will we ensure that measurement information is used as the basis for *feedback?*
- How will we ensure that measurement information is used as the basis for *rewards?*
- How will we ensure that measurement information is an input to *performance appraisal, career development, and promotion?*
- How will we ensure that our measures and goals are *current* (that is, that they reflect today's business conditions)?

If measures capture the right dimensions of the right performance, a measurement system should achieve these objectives:

- Maximize information *accuracy.*
- Optimize the *volume* of information (not too much or too little).
- Maximize *usefulness* as a performance management tool.
- Maximize *timeliness* (not too delayed to be actionable).
- Maximize ease of *understanding.*
- Minimize information collection *cost and time.*
- Minimize opportunities for *"beating the system."*

In spite of her reservations about measurement, Ellen—the district manager introduced at the beginning of this chapter—is pleased with the way Fill Your Tank is going about the measurement system initiative.

The process began at the top, with the executive team reviewing and updating the corporate strategy. As part of this exercise, they established strategic measures and goals, which include:

- **Revenue of $210M in four years, $175M in three years, $140M in two years, and $120M next year. In all years, net income should exceed 12 percent.**
- **Twenty percent annual growth in same-store sales.**
- **Six new stores opened per year.**
- **Thirty percent share of the convenience business in the target markets identified in the strategy.**

- Twenty-five percent growth in the number of customers who buy gasoline along with their convenience store purchases.
- Twenty percent of stores contain a fast food franchise (a new business for Fill Your Tank) within four years. $25M in fast food revenue by the fourth year of the strategy.
- Eighty percent "Excellent" and "Good" ratings in all Customer Satisfaction Survey categories.

The top team supplemented these strategic measures with a set of companywide operational measures:

- Employee retention rates above local average in all markets.
- Shrinkage (losses due to theft) less than 0.5 percent in all districts.
- No more than one minor health inspection violation per store per year.
- All employees receive at least three days of customer service training per year.

Based on the strategy, the top team identified inventory management, staff scheduling, and customer service as their core processes. Following the steps outlined in Table 6.1, they identified performance dimensions, measures, and goals for each process. For example (see Table 6.2):

Table 6.2 Fill Your Tank Inventory Management Process Measures

Performance Dimension	Measure	Goal
Quality	Number of products with stock-outs (empty shelves) within store control at any given time (based on routine "secret shopper" visits)	≤ 6 products
Cost	Percent of revenue of stock destroyed or returned by each store due to spoilage or date expiration	≤ 2 percent
Cycle Time	Order-to-receipt time for fad, impulse-buy products	≤ 6 business days

Based on the strategic goals, the companywide operational goals, and the end-of-process and upstream goals for both core and non-core processes, district goals were set. To ensure that these goals were realistic and had the commitment of the district managers, Ellen and her peers participated in this process. A team of district managers and store managers then developed the metrics that would be used to assess store and individual job performance. Then they developed and installed a process in which district and store managers establish goals for each store.

Lastly, the Performance Enhancement staff—with input from all levels—developed an automated measurement system that captures, displays, and communicates actual performance information compared to goals at all levels. They were careful to balance completeness and practicality, to ensure that the measurement information was available to the right people at the right time, and to link the job measures to human resources processes like performance evaluation and promotion.

Goal setting is part vision, part mechanics. The design, installation, and maintenance of a measurement system certainly falls into the category of management, as opposed to leadership (see Chapter 3). However, that should not relegate it to second-class citizenship. With the right measurement system, you can identify needs in all of the other components of the Enterprise Model. Surfacing gaps is the first step in improvement.

■ NOTE

1. R. Kaplan and D. Norton, *The Balanced Scorecard: Translating Strategy into Action* (Boston: Harvard Business School Press, 1996).

Reframing Culture

Glenn Macfarland had read the statistics about merger/acquisition failures, but he thought he could beat the odds. The CEO of Ridgedale Paper had identified what appeared to be the perfect acquisition candidate, Plymouth Fiber.

- Their product lines were synergistic, with minimal overlap.
- They served the same markets and, in some cases, the same customers.
- They had complementary manufacturing capabilities.
- The Plymouth CEO was about to retire, so there would be no need to pick a winner or set up an artificial and confusing co-CEO structure.
- The federal regulators had no antitrust concerns.
- Due diligence surfaced no insurmountable legal, environmental, or accounting issues.
- Because the companies' administrative offices were geographically proximate, moving people was not a concern. Glenn did not see a need to reduce headcount, other than through normal attrition.
- The price was right for both parties.

The deal was closed relatively quickly. The first few months of the marriage met all of Glenn's expectations, perhaps because the companies ran autonomously and people were in a wait-and-see mode. But then, as integration actions began to be taken, the dark clouds started forming.

- A Ridgedale executive dismissed Plymouth's informal atmosphere as "summer camp" and accused one of its mill managers of "understanding paper but not understanding business." The Plymouth contingent is bristling at the formality of Ridgedale practices and openly refers to its managers as "b-school bean counters."
- Ridgedale has a marketing and finance orientation. Plymouth is driven by engineering and production. What appeared to be complementary strengths have turned out to be the basis of dysfunctional clashes. Even though the two companies are in the same business, they do not speak the same language.
- While the executive responsibilities were established without much pain, lower-level job definition was surfacing some substantive, friction-inducing differences. For example, Ridgedale and Plymouth have fundamentally disparate views of the role of management and incongruent philosophies regarding whether product quality should be designed in or inspected in.
- Plymouth has a team structure; Ridgedale is built around individual superstars. Ridgedale relies on data; Plymouth relies on intuition. Plymouth builds relationships; Ridgedale sells products. Ridgedale's pace is frenetic; Plymouth's is leisurely.

Glenn failed to look behind the alarmingly high acquisition failure rate statistics. The cause of most failures is not strategic misalignment, financial overextension, market confusion, or even power struggles in the executive suite. It is cultural incompatibility.

One way to define and analyze a business is in terms of "what" and "how."

- Strategy defines *what* business an organization will be in and *how* it is going to win.
- Business Processes define *what* is done at the operational level (for example, the steps in mortgage loan processing, the steps in Web site development, the steps in wholesaler invoicing). They also document the *structural* aspects of *how* a process is carried out, such as the role of each department, the content and format of documents, and the support provided by information systems.
- Job descriptions define *what* is expected from individuals and teams in a business process. In most cases, they should

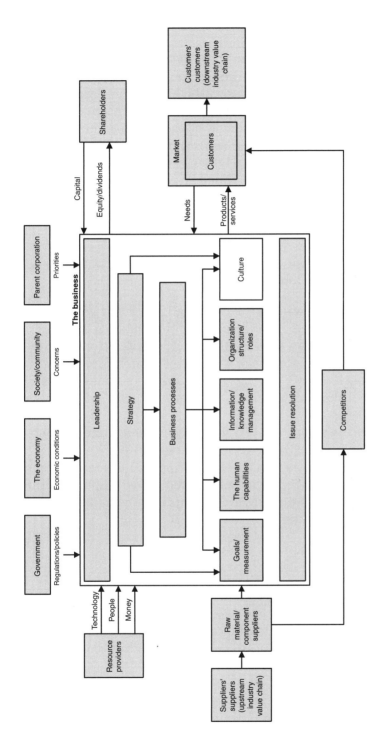

Figure 7.1 The Position of Culture in the Enterprise Model

101

contain outputs, but should *not* specify the *how,* which is the behaviors that produce the outputs. For example, you want salespeople to develop forecasts, but may not want to specify every step they take en route. You expect store managers to ensure adequate coverage of each department, but may not want to legislate their scheduling methods.

For responsibilities in which both outputs and behaviors are critical (for example, nuclear power plant maintenance and focus group information collection), the job description is still the "what." "Conformance to policies and procedures" can be one of the goals.

There is another level of "how" that permeates all business processes and the jobs within them. For example:

- A process shows when a meeting is held and who attends; however, it does not indicate how that meeting is run.
- A process shows where and who makes decisions, but does not display the degree to which risk is considered.
- A process shows the types and timing of communication, but not the way in which that communication is delivered or received.
- A process shows when a form is completed and by whom, but not how seriously people take it.
- A process shows that the Marketing and Research Departments work together to define product development priorities, but it does not provide insights into the nature and tone of their interaction.

This level of "how" is culture.

■ WHAT IS CULTURE?

Culture is the values, rules, practices, rituals, and norms through which you conduct business. Simply, it is the way you do things. For example:

- To what degree do executives tolerate mistakes?
- How much and what type of financial information is shared?
- To what degree do employees trust management?

- How do people get ongoing feedback on their performance?
- How do people communicate?
- What is the pace?
- To what degree is innovation supported?
- What is the level of risk tolerance?
- What performance is rewarded?
- Are people externally focused or internally focused?
- Where does the real power lie?
- What is the dress code?

Strategy delineates the boundaries of your organization's pond; culture is the water in which you swim.

■ WHY IS CULTURE IMPORTANT?

Culture is important because of its profound influence on strategy formulation, strategy implementation, and employee satisfaction.

An enlightened culture cannot substitute for a clear strategy. Remember PeopleExpress Airlines? It had a model culture that was described in case studies, lauded in articles, and enshrined as a benchmarking Mecca. It went out of business because its executives failed to establish a clear position in the industry. In terms of the breakdown at the beginning of this chapter, PeopleExpress nailed the "how" but died because it lacked a viable "what."

On the other hand, a clear strategy can only be implemented through an aligned culture. For example:

- If your business is to grow through new products, you need a culture of innovation.
- If you are going to win through world-class after-sale service, you must have a customer-focused culture.
- If you are going to be in fashion footwear, one of your cultural attributes had better be speed.
- If you are pursuing a low-cost-producer strategy, thriftiness ought to permeate not only your manufacturing and distribution operations but also your office facilities, meeting locations, company-funded social events, and modes of transportation.

- If you are going to sell proprietary software, your culture needs to attract and retain first-class application developers.
- If your primary business is to supply components to the automotive industry, your culture should be one in which people eat, sleep, and breathe cars.

Because culture is an essential ingredient in successful strategy implementation, it should be a key factor in the selection of your strategic direction. In a pivotal strategy formulation activity (see Chapter 4), your organization's executives should evaluate distinct alternatives and select the best path for your business. Since culture can change, cultural congruence should not be a filter for potential strategies. However, because culture change is a long-term process, "compatibility with current culture" should be one of the selection criteria.

Research[1] has shown that there is a high correlation between customer satisfaction and employee satisfaction. Happy employees tend to create happy customers. The primary influence on employee satisfaction is cultural factors such as the decision-making authority people are given, the degree of respect for individuals, the way people are treated, the performance that is rewarded, the flexibility of work schedule and location, and the voice people are given in structuring their work environment.

Satisfied employees produce better products, offer better services, and make the customer's interface with the organization more pleasant. When a customer contact person is unhappy with his or her job, customers (1) notice and (2) wonder what is wrong with the company.

■ WHAT ARE THE CHARACTERISTICS OF CULTURE?

It is impossible to cover all conceivable dimensions of culture. Here is a start:

- Open or guarded
- Risk tolerant or risk averse
- Fast paced or plodding
- Fact based or intuition based
- Customer focused or internally focused
- Trusting or suspicious
- Candid or duplicitous
- Innovative or tradition bound
- Analytical or emotional
- Strategic or tactical

- Analog or digital
- Clear or ambiguous
- Social or asocial
- All work or work-life balanced
- Formal or casual
- Visionary or projective
- Internally competitive or collaborative
- Political or apolitical
- Polite or confrontational
- Change seeking or change resistant
- Protocol oriented or freewheeling
- Flexible or rigid
- Autocratic or participative
- Progressive or conservative
- Leading or following
- Stimulating or boring
- Caring or uncaring
- Optimistic or pessimistic
- Arrogant or humble

- Hungry or satisfied
- Lone ranger or team oriented
- High control or laissez-faire
- Values driven or situational
- Loyal or disloyal
- Critical or supportive
- Plan focused or execution focused
- Quality driven or cost driven
- Aggressive or passive
- Humorous or serious
- Focused or diffused
- Secure or insecure
- People oriented or thing oriented
- Fun or tedious
- Entrepreneurial or business-as-usual
- Rewarding or punishing
- Thrifty or profligate
- Tolerant or intolerant
- Short-term or long-term

The "or" in some of these pairs can be misleading. For example, the healthiest answer to "Are we quality driven or cost driven?" and "Are we plan focused or execution focused?" is "Yes."

In some organizations, the apt adjective differs, depending on the situation or the part of the business being examined. Some organizations are a mélange of cultures, which may be appropriate or—like the paper company cited at the beginning of this chapter—dysfunctional.

■ WHAT ROLE DOES COMMUNICATION PLAY IN AN ORGANIZATION'S CULTURE?

Communication is an especially important dimension of culture because it has such a profound influence on the success of the other variables in the Enterprise Model.

- Communication is central to a number of the roles played by leaders: inspiring, mobilizing, cheerleading, and energizing (see Chapter 3).
- A significant component of *strategy* implementation—some argue the *most* significant component—is the clear, compelling communication of values, vision, and priorities (see Chapter 4).
- Most of what moves through *business processes*—even in a manufacturing operation—is not tangible products but information (see Chapter 5).
- The way *goals* are communicated has a major influence not only on the degree to which they are understood but also on the degree to which they are embraced, tolerated, or resisted (see Chapter 6).
- Oral and written communication skills are key *capabilities* in most jobs (see Chapter 8).
- Communication of the "what," "why," and "how" is crucial to the successful implementation of *information systems* (see Chapter 9) and *organization structures* (see Chapter 10).
- Communication of facts and opinions is a vital component of *issue resolution* (see Chapter 11).

Communication provides a particularly wide window into an organization's culture, as evidenced by these questions:

- Is most communication formal or informal?
- Is most communication one way or two way?
- Is most communication brief or lengthy? In other words, do we have a Calvin Coolidge culture or a Fidel Castro culture? (For those who are not students of American history, Coolidge was a legendarily taciturn president. When an admirer told "Silent Cal" that she bet a friend that she could get him to say more than two words, the President responded, "You lose." Castro, on the other hand, can give a five-hour speech at the drop of a cigar ash.)
- In most communication, what is the mix between the factual and the emotional?
- How much communication is done via pictures (charts, models, graphs, cartoons) as opposed to merely words?
- What kinds of communication are written and what kinds are oral?

- Do people tend to communicate via voice mail, e-mail, paper memo, voice-to-voice, or face-to-face?
- What is the communication dynamic in meetings? (Who communicates? to whom? why? how often? in what way?)
- Is communication to outsiders (customers, suppliers, investors, regulators) different from that within the organization? in what ways? why?
- In general, is the nature/tone/medium of communication more important than the message, as important as the message, or less important than the message?
- To what degree is communication adapted to the style of the recipients? Do people, perhaps aided by Myers-Briggs®, identify and address other people's communication needs?

Communication is not merely words or pictures; it includes facial expressions, eye contact, gestures, proximity, body configuration (for example, open or closed), and even the setting in which the communication occurs.

If you understand communication patterns, norms, and styles, you have covered a significant portion of the cultural waterfront.

■ WHAT DETERMINES CULTURE?

An organization's culture is determined by its:

- *Current leadership.* A scan of the list in "What Are the Characteristics of Culture?" will enable you to identify the personality, biases, and style of your organization's leaders (see Chapter 3). As people learn about their leaders, they tend to begin adapting their characteristics. When critical mass is achieved, it becomes woven into the culture and takes on a life beyond the leader.

  The influence of current leadership on culture is not limited to larger-than-life figures like IBM's Thomas Watson, Chrysler's Lee Iacocca, or GE's Jack Welch. Any person in power exerts significant cultural impact.

  For example, if a leader requires factual backup for recommendations that are brought to him, his managers tend to require the same level of rigor in proposals brought to them. If a leader is risk averse, her organization tends to be risk averse. If a leader has a work hard/play hard orientation, the organization tends to adapt that culture.

In situations in which the leader is not respected, people respond to their leader's proclivities by rebelling against, rather than adopting, them. If the leader is humorless, they make jokes. If the leader likes voice mails, they send e-mails. If the leader is pursuing change, they defend the status quo. This condition tends to be temporary; either the leader adapts, the followers adapt, or someone leaves.

Regardless of whether they stimulate consistent or contrary behaviors, leaders' viewpoints and actions are a major influence—healthy or unhealthy—on the culture.

- *Founders.* Even if the torch of an organization's leadership has passed from the original founders, their imprint on the culture can last for generations. Examples:

  ➤ McDonald's founder Ray Kroc's philosophy of the fast food experience.

  ➤ Hallmark founder Joyce Hall's "Good taste is good business."[2]

  ➤ Walt Disney's credos of family entertainment.

  ➤ Sam Walton's tenets of how Wal-Mart's customers and employees should be treated.

  ➤ Bill Hewlett and Dave Packard's focus on innovation.

  ➤ Akito Morita of Sony's passion for discovering needs that consumers do not realize they have.

  ➤ Southwest Airlines' Herb Kelleher's fascination with employee fun as a route to customer satisfaction.

- *Strategy.* While the personalities of individual leaders and founders have a significant influence on culture, so do the strategies that those leaders have established. For example:

  ➤ Nordstrom's strategy focuses on attracting and retaining clientele through customer service that exceeds expectations. The culture of that department store chain is characterized by a fixation on service.

➤ Federal Express's strategy is to "absolutely, positively" meet its delivery time commitments. Speed is not only an obsession of its drivers but of its employees in all positions and at all levels.

➤ Yahoo!'s strategy includes making the Internet fun for its customers. Part of the implementation of that strategy is through the playful environment that it creates for its employees.

▪ *Customers.* Just as dogs and their masters tend to look like each other, suppliers tend to adopt the culture of their customers. The jargon, the dress, the operating style, the priorities, and the look and feel of the culture all tend to mirror that of their primary customer. For example:

➤ If you walk the halls of Lockheed Martin, you would swear that you are in a NASA or Department of Defense installation.

➤ Home Depot employees look and sound like the building contractors that represent one of their target customer groups.

➤ BMW's culture reflects the yuppies to whom they sell. You will not find any polyester suits on their employees, bowling on their sales meeting agendas, or muscatel in their cafeterias.

■ HOW CAN YOU UNDERSTAND YOUR CULTURE?

Just as in the ancient civilizations studied by anthropologists, organization culture is evident in its artifacts. Mission statements, policy documents, plans, memos, training programs, job descriptions, business cards, and bulletin board notices all give insight into culture.

Unlike the Sumerians' or the Druids', your organization's culture still exists; as a result, you can go beyond artifacts to learn through observation. Attire, the layout and decoration of the workspace, and the cars (or bicycles or scooters) people drive provide further evidence of the prevailing folkways. Watching the nature, location, and duration of informal human interactions—in the halls, by the coffee machine, in the parking lot—is illuminating. Whenever possible, sit in on various types of meetings; they tend to be a microcosm of the culture.

Interviewing and surveying employees at all levels (and, if possible, customers and suppliers) provide further evidence of an organization's personality. The words that are used and nonverbal cues during interviews are often as revealing as the message.

One of the most powerful insights into culture comes from the stories that pass from generation to generation. Some are true; some are myth. But they communicate the norms that underpin the business.

- When hiring for key positions, Henry Ford's selection process reputedly included taking candidates to dinner. If they put salt or pepper on their food before tasting it, he would not make them an offer. He did not want executives who made decisions without facts. True? It does not matter; the story established a dimension of the Ford culture.
- Microsoft employees and suppliers tell stories about Bill Gates's public humiliations of those who cannot make their way across the intellectual minefields he creates for them. Even though he has reportedly mellowed since he began breeding, the stories live on.
- The FedEx culture is influenced by the stories of beyond-the-call-of-duty efforts of drivers who overcame floods and pestilence to deliver packages on time.
- A legend was created in a law firm when a partner flew from New York to Los Angeles and logged 27 billable hours for that day.

■ CAN CULTURE CHANGE?

Culture can change. For example:

- Nokia transformed itself from a stodgy Finnish smokestack conglomerate to a fast-paced global telecommunications powerhouse.
- GE, under the same CEO, has evolved from financially driven and uncaring to values driven and humanistic. The

company has focused on its people without taking its eyes off the numbers.
- Barnes and Noble is one of the small number of traditional retailers that have successfully immersed themselves in the ways of the Internet.

Cultural transformation is usually measured in years rather than months. The executive who wants a cultural sea change by the end of the quarter is likely to be disappointed. The length of the journey is a function of the degree of change and the depth of the roots.

Figure 7.2 displays a simple change process. This process applies to any change, from moving an office to launching a new advertising campaign to hiring a group of people to introducing a new product. However, these steps are more complex, more stressful, and more time consuming for culture transformation than for any other change, with the possible exceptions of entering an entirely new business or exiting a business with deep roots.

Before embarking on a culture transformation, you may want to take a step back and ask these questions:

- Why do you want to change the culture?
- Might other variables in the Enterprise Model more quickly and inexpensively achieve the same objectives?
- What is the constituency for change? In other words, who in the organization sees the need for a culture transformation? (If it is just the chief executive, that is a far different environment from one in which nearly everyone perceives the current culture as a weak platform on which to build the future.)
- How will you know if the cultural transformation has occurred?
- How much time and money are you willing to invest in the transformation process depicted in Figure 7.2?

■ WHAT ARE TYPICAL WEAKNESSES IN CULTURE?

It is difficult to imagine a business in which a culture of venality or customer abuse would be desirable. However, within reasonable boundaries, a culture is neither right nor wrong in the

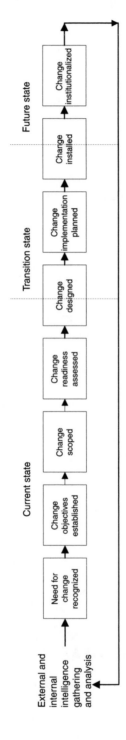

Figure 7.2 A Process for Managing Change

absolute. An organization's culture needs to be congruent with its unique situation. Your culture is deficient if

- It does not fit your *strategy* or the business processes that translate that strategy into operations. A controlled-growth strategy requires a different culture than a through-the-roof-growth culture. A market-share-at-all-costs strategy requires a different culture than a profit-is-king strategy. A strategy in which manufacturing capability is the primary competitive advantage should spawn a different culture than one in which manufacturing is outsourced and advantages lie elsewhere.
- It does not appeal to and support your core *employees*. A buttoned-down, formal culture probably does not support fashion designers or programmers. A paperwork-intensive environment does not appeal to most executive-level sales representatives. A penurious, risk-averse culture is unlikely to get the best from entrepreneurs and dealmakers.
- It is not aligned with the culture of your *customers*. A boorish culture does not go down well with Japanese customers.

➤ SELF-ASSESSMENT QUESTIONS

Culture is the product of behaviors and attitudes. Behaviors and attitudes are a function of employees' interpretation of, evaluation of, and response to the cultural influences depicted in Figure 7.3.

A hard-sell culture tends to make regulated utility buyers uncomfortable. A low-key, cerebral culture may not be appropriate if your market is professional wrestling fans.

Let us say that you want innovation—product innovation, customer relationship innovation, process innovation—to be one of the hallmarks of your culture. Asking the cultural influence questions in Figure 7.3 will help you understand whether people in key positions:

- Understand and agree with the strategic need for innovation.
- Understand the types of innovations that are expected from them.

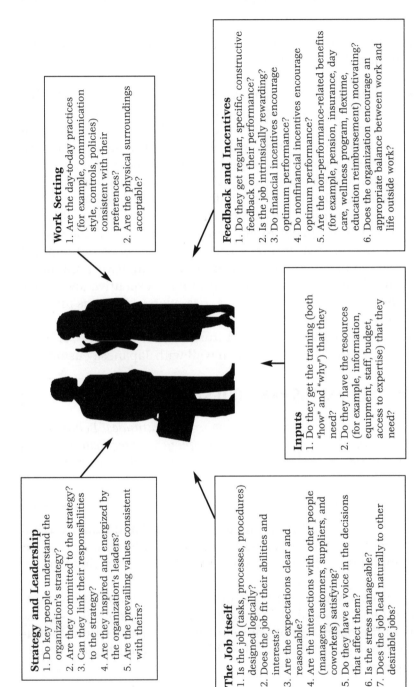

Strategy and Leadership
1. Do key people understand the organization's strategy?
2. Are they committed to the strategy?
3. Can they link their responsibilities to the strategy?
4. Are they inspired and energized by the organization's leaders?
5. Are the prevailing values consistent with theirs?

Work Setting
1. Are the day-to-day practices (for example, communication style, controls, policies) consistent with their preferences?
2. Are the physical surroundings acceptable?

The Job Itself
1. Is the job (tasks, processes, procedures) designed logically?
2. Does the job fit their abilities and interests?
3. Are the expectations clear and reasonable?
4. Are the interactions with other people (managers, customers, suppliers, and coworkers) satisfying?
5. Do they have a voice in the decisions that affect them?
6. Is the stress manageable?
7. Does the job lead naturally to other desirable jobs?

Inputs
1. Do they get the training (both "how" and "why") that they need?
2. Do they have the resources (for example, information, equipment, staff, budget, access to expertise) that they need?

Feedback and Incentives
1. Do they get regular, specific, constructive feedback on their performance?
2. Is the job intrinsically rewarding?
3. Do financial incentives encourage optimum performance?
4. Do nonfinancial incentives encourage optimum performance?
5. Are the non-performance-related benefits (for example, pension, insurance, day care, wellness program, flextime, education reimbursement) motivating?
6. Does the organization encourage an appropriate balance between work and life outside work?

Figure 7.3 The Cultural Influences

- Have the training and tools to innovate.
- Work in a physical setting that supports innovation.
- Get feedback on their innovations.
- Are rewarded for innovating.

Every question that is answered "no" or "sometimes" is a chink in the cultural armor. You can use these questions to take the temperature of a culture and to unearth the root causes of deficiencies in the culture.

These same questions can also be used to troubleshoot individual and group performance problems. In a sales organization, for example, they can help you identify the factors contributing to the lack of business in a certain industry, late submission of forecasts, or selling product A rather than the higher-margin product B.

■ WHAT IS THE PROCESS FOR ADDRESSING THE CULTURE VARIABLE?

The steps in tackling the culture dimension of your enterprise are:

1. Using the descriptors in "What Are the Characteristics of Culture?" as thought starters, profile the culture that best supports your strategy. The parts of your strategy (see Chapter 4) that serve as the primary culture drivers are your values and beliefs; your statement of competitive advantage(s); your sources of growth (new products, new markets, new businesses); and the capabilities (processes, people, equipment, facilities) required for success.

   As described at the outset of this chapter, Glenn Macfarland's challenge was to transform Ridgedale and Plymouth into Ridgedale Plymouth, not just in name, but in practice. He realized that as long as he did not have a clear statement of future product scope and emphasis, market scope and emphasis, and particularly values and competitive advantage, he lacked a cultural compass. So, his first step was to establish a strategy that answered the questions in Chapter 4.

Glenn and his new executive team formulated a three-year Ridgedale Plymouth strategy, the cornerstones of which were:

➤ An emphasis on customized paper and cardboard products.

➤ An emphasis on packaging applications for business customers.

➤ A boundaryless approach to customers and the deployment of Ridgedale Plymouth resources.

➤ Winning though price and the depth and breadth of relationships.

Based on the strategy, they developed a profile of the future culture that required it to be:

➤ Entrepreneurial.

➤ Nimble.

➤ Customer focused.

➤ Risk taking, but always with a sound business case.

➤ Cost conscious.

2. Via surveys, interviews, observation, and the review of artifacts, define your current culture. Again, "What Are the Characteristics of Culture?" can be your guide.

Glenn Macfarland's problem was that he had two cultures. More formal information collection led to some new insights and validated the anecdotal data. Each legacy company contributed to some dimensions of the new culture and had to extinguish aspects of its current culture. For example, Ridgedale could teach Plymouth lessons about cost consciousness and speed. Plymouth could migrate its relationship management skills and flexibility.

3. Identify the highest-priority gaps between your current culture and the culture required by your strategy.

Ridgedale Plymouth's highest-priority culture gaps were:

➤ Lack of flexibility, which was essential to the custom products business and was not a hallmark of either company.

➤ Absence of entrepreneurship. Below the top level, both companies were populated by specialists, not by rounded businesspeople.

➤ Absence of a cost mentality among the Plymouth people.

➤ Absence of customer focus among the Ridgedale people.

➤ Employees' general lack of trust of and respect for individuals from the other company.

4. Identify the key positions in your organization. (Your strategy and business processes should direct this activity. Does your business revolve around your field service engineers? your tellers? your call center personnel? your chemists? your ad copywriters? your application developers? your product managers?)

The top team identified the following nonmanagerial positions as most pivotal to the implementation of Ridgedale Plymouth's strategy:

➤ Packaging consultants, the new name for the people who were responsible for business development and custom solution configuration.

➤ Product engineers, who were responsible for designing the products that the packaging consultants sell.

➤ Financial analysts, who formulated prices and ensured that cost efficiencies enabled Ridgedale Plymouth to maintain its price advantage.

5. Diagnose the cultural influences on these key positions by asking the questions in Figure 7.3.

An analysis of the cultural influences on Ridgedale Plymouth's financial analysts surfaced some revealing "no" answers. One of the key expectations—initiating cost improvement actions, as opposed to merely reporting on cost performance—had never been clearly communicated. Furthermore, their incentives drove the wrong behavior. Analysts occasionally received management praise for establishing prices that achieved margin targets. However, that praise was less frequent and powerful than the negative consequences they got from packaging consultants who perceived price as a barrier to closing a piece of business.

6. Determine what actions you should take to convert every "no" answer in Step 5 to "yes."

The management of the Finance Department clarified the financial analysts' cost improvement expectations. They concluded that the analysts' disincentives for establishing margin-protecting prices were due to packaging consultants' perception that pricing was a black art that was unique to each situation. A team of finance managers and analysts documented the pricing policies, process, and formulas and communicated them to the consultants.

Since the packaging consultant and product engineer positions had been substantially reconfigured, the questions in Figure 7.3 were not used to identify weaknesses in their current environment. They were used to *design* an ideal work climate (to create "yes" answers from the start). For example, since flexibility was going to be a competitive advantage, managers put in place clear expectations regarding flexibility, adequate resources for flexibility, supportive feedback on flexibility, and incentives that encouraged flexibility.

7. Lay out a plan, including responsibilities and realistic time frames, for taking the actions identified in Step 6. As you develop and implement your plan, consider the steps in the change process depicted in Figure 7.2.

8. Test your plan against the gaps that you identified in Step 3. For any needs that are not addressed, add gap-closing actions.

9. Implement the plan, making midcourse corrections as needed.

Like leadership, culture is a theme throughout the other variables in the Enterprise Model. All of the effort you put into designing the structural variables—*business processes, goals/ measurement, information/knowledge management,* and *organization structure/roles*—can be undercut by weaknesses in your culture. Defining the culture that you need to implement your strategy and following the diagnostic/action-planning process outlined above are essential steps in creating a world-class enterprise.

■ NOTES

1. American Productivity and Quality Center, "Leveraging Call Center Investments to Enhance Customer Satisfaction," 1999; and Best Practices, LLC, "Best Practices in Customer and Employee Satisfaction Management," 2000.
2. *Forbes, 13* November 2000, 250.

Chapter 8

Managing Human Capabilities

Susan Billingham does not have clear priorities. For some of her projects, she is not even sure what she is being asked to do. For two of her key assignments, she understands and supports the intent, but does not agree with the approach that she is being asked to take. Other than that, everything is okay.

Susan is the vice president of human resources for Customerge, a venture capital-funded Silicon Valley start-up company. Customerge has developed and launched a suite of software packages that connect suppliers and customers, multiple sites within a company, and remote employees, such as field sales and service representatives. Susan is a veteran human resources professional who was lured to Customerge with a hefty compensation package that includes generous stock options. She has been on board since the company opened its doors 18 months ago.

As is typical in a start-up situation, Susan is not burdened with defective processes and practices; her challenge is the absence of processes and practices. The founders and other key players are software development whizzes who have little patience for the nitty-gritty of business protocols, organization structure, job descriptions, benefit plans, and career development. The root of Susan's frustration is her perception that she is being asked to set up systems in an environment that has no tolerance for them. Every time she proposes something that smacks of "old economy" formality, her colleagues on the executive committee look heavenward, pull out their personal digital assistants and start responding to e-mails. A recent comment from the vice president of operations typified the prevailing mindset: "Susan, just hire bright people; we will find a place for them."

Whenever a people issue comes up, they throw it into Susan's lap. Within the last month, she has been asked to:

- Recruit six new programmers.
- Create a culture that retains existing talent.
- Establish a competitive compensation plan.
- Give people workplace benefits "like other progressive companies in the Valley."
- Ensure that people have whatever training they need.
- Identify the people who have the interest and aptitude for the management jobs that are being created as the organization grows.

Susan needs to establish her own priorities, rather than being buffeted by the winds of the other executives' issues du jour. She needs to make recommendations that are more compelling to her colleagues. To achieve these two objectives, Susan requires a framework for building Customerge's human capabilities.

You can have a boatload of market and competitive research and a powerful strategy formulation process. However, a strategy is only as good as the people who create it. Its implementation plan is only as good as the people who develop it. Its deployment is only as good as the people who manage and staff the projects in the plan.

Business processes can be well designed, codified, International Organization for Standardization (ISO) certified, and digitally enabled. However, at their essence, processes are "people doing things."

A manufacturing operation can be automated with state-of-the-art robots and computer-controlled equipment. But that plant is only as good as the people who design it, maintain it, and manage it.

■ WHAT ARE HUMAN CAPABILITIES?

As depicted in Figure 8.2, human capabilities are the skills, knowledge, and personal values/beliefs of the people who

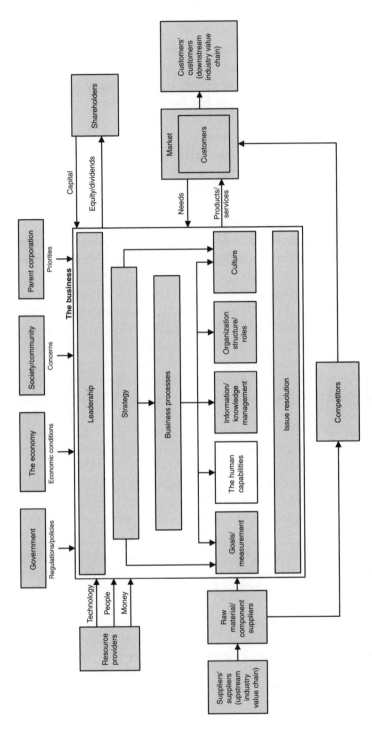

Figure 8.1 The Position of Human Capabilities in the Enterprise Model

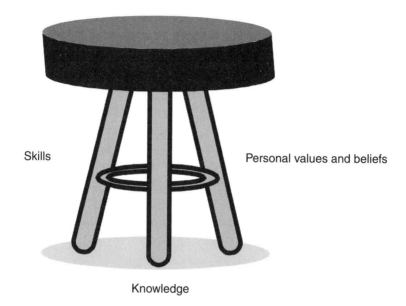

Skills

Personal values and beliefs

Knowledge

Figure 8.2 The Three Types of Human Capabilities

perform tasks in the work environment. Human capabilities meld with process design capabilities, equipment capabilities, leadership, and culture to produce results.

Repair people, customer service representatives, receptionists, call center staff, machine operators, and retail checkout people work within processes. Because they function as individuals a large percentage of the time, they can successfully play their roles in those processes only if they have a full complement of capabilities.

However, in an increasing number of processes—assembly, warehousing, research and development, construction, auditing, sales, consulting—work is carried out by teams. In those settings, no individual is expected to have the complete repertoire of capabilities. As long as the requisite skills and knowledge are resident in the team and deployed when and where they are needed, the process can meet its goals.

For a given process step, a list of human capabilities answers four simple-but-critical questions:

- Who should be involved in this step?
- What do they have to know?

- What do they have to be able to do?
- What values and beliefs do they have to have?

■ HOW DO YOU IDENTIFY THE HUMAN CAPABILITIES YOU NEED?

Ultimately, human capability needs are defined by an organization's strategy. As discussed in Chapter 4, your strategy may spell out the capabilities—human, business process, equipment, facilities—that you need to establish your competitive advantages. If your strategy does not list and describe your human capability requirements, it should be specific enough to enable you to derive them, using the links in the chain presented in Figure 8.3.

Table 8.1 includes four examples of this flow from strategy to human capabilities. For simplicity, each example includes just one aspect of the strategy and a single process, department, and job requirement.

The first four columns of Table 8.1 should serve as the springboards for the strategic, process, department, and job goals discussed in Chapter 6.

Not all human capabilities directly fuel a strategic objective. While every job output—and therefore every skill and knowledge—ought to contribute to the strategy in some way, the links are not always as clear as in the Table 8.1 examples. For example, the people in Human Resources who process benefit claims, the people in Facilities who manage the telephone system, and the people in Maintenance who service equipment perform important functions that only tangentially feed the strategy. To get at the capabilities in these areas, you begin by identifying the business process requirements and then follow the rest of the sequence.

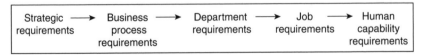

Figure 8.3 Human Capability Needs Identification

Table 8.1 Examples of Human Capabilities

Strategic Requirement	Business Process Requirement	Department Requirement	Job Requirement	Human Capability Requirements
Product scope: We will offer only differentiated products.	Inventory management process: Inventory of commodity products eliminated	Finance department: Balance sheet impact managed	Financial Analyst: Write-offs calculated	• Write-off policies • Basic math • Depreciation formulas • Accounting rules • Spreadsheet entry and data manipulation
Product emphasis: We will emphasize after-sale services.	Business development process: Service business grown	Sales department: Service contracts sold	National Account Relationship Manager: Long-term service contracts sold to national accounts	• National account needs and buying criteria • Product benefits and features • Pricing policies • Listening • Relationship building
Thrust for growth: Our primary growth will come from offering existing products to new markets.	Market entry process: Desirability of potential markets ranked	Marketing department: Market size, competition, and likely price point researched	Market Research Specialist: Target customers profiled	• Demographic data collection and analysis • Psychographic data collection and analysis • Microeconomic analysis • Customer profile format
Competitive advantage: We will win through the rapid development and launch of customized products.	Product development process: Products rapidly prototyped	Engineering department: Mock-ups designed and constructed	Engineer: Mock-up specifications written	• Functionality assessment • CAD/CAM design protocols • Technical writing • Nontechnical writing • Budget guidelines • Cross-functional collaboration

■ HOW DO BEHAVIORS RELATE TO HUMAN CAPABILITIES?

Now that we have looked upstream at the strategic and process requirements that determine human capability needs, let us look more closely at the links to and from human capabilities.

You may find value in documenting a step between job requirements and human capability requirements: *behaviors.* Job requirements are documented in output terms and those outputs should be measured. However, an output is produced through one or more behaviors or activities.

For example, the national account relationship managers cited in Table 8.1 sell long-term service contracts through behaviors such as (1) developing a sales plan for each customer (whom to contact, when to contact them, how to approach the sale); (2) identifying the service contract benefits and features that will be most attractive to each customer; (3) setting up appointments for face-to-face sales calls; (4) meeting with prospects; (5) identifying the terms and conditions that should be in the service contracts; (6) determining prices; (7) developing and submitting proposed contracts; (8) presenting proposals; and (9) closing sales.

This simple list of activities illustrates the behaviors that lead to the result, which is the sale of long-term service contracts. Identifying these behaviors may help us identify the human capabilities that national account relationship managers need. For example, they need:

- *Knowledge,* such as the content and format of a sales plan, the benefits and features of the product, and the boundaries within which customized contracts must fall.
- *Skills,* such as discovering needs, making presentations, and negotiating terms.
- *Values and beliefs,* such as passion for the product, fervent belief in its price-value relationship, and a customer-centered orientation to all parts of their job.

In addition to helping with human capability definition, identifying behaviors helps you troubleshoot substandard performance. When salespeople fail to meet their targets, we can look for the root cause in their behaviors. Are they not getting in front of the right people? not thoroughly probing for needs? not clearly describing the benefits of the service? not quoting an appropriate price?

Similarly, behaviors help you understand *top* performers. Salespeople who consistently outperform their colleagues may be:

- Doing things that others are not (for example, developing customer-specific sales literature).
- Doing things differently (for example, always presenting proposals face-to-face, rather than sending them in the mail).
- Doing things better (for example, using a computer-projected menu of possible benefits during the discovery part of a sales call).

By drilling down to the behavior level, you can develop a deep understanding of performance. Based on that understanding, you can create a comprehensive list of the skills, knowledge, and values/beliefs that are required for exemplary performance.

Illuminating as behaviors can be, you do not want to fall in the trap of measuring behaviors rather than results. Salespeople can do an exemplary job of developing sales plans, setting up appointments, building relationships, writing proposals, and making presentations. However, they are paid to close business, and that is how they should be measured.

■ WHAT INDIVIDUAL ABILITIES AND ATTRIBUTES INFLUENCE SKILLS AND KNOWLEDGE?

Just as taking the lid off outputs reveals behaviors, if you look underneath human capabilities, you can see performers' innate abilities and attributes. These aspects of an individual's persona—on which organizations have limited influence—fall into three categories:

- Physical (for example, strength, dexterity, and stamina).
- Intellectual (for example, analytical ability, creativity, and memory).

- Psychological (for example, personality traits, emotional makeup, and motivators).

One could make a case for these three factors directly influencing behaviors and, ultimately, outputs; however, it is more practical to see them as influencing skills and knowledge.

Here are some examples of *physical barriers* to skill development:

- An appliance assembly worker may have all of the knowledge and desire necessary to perform the nonautomated part of the job but lack the manual dexterity to insert the components in the proper place.
- A warehouse worker may lack the strength to operate forklift levers or align boxes on a pallet.
- A retail clerk may have a condition that prevents her from standing on her feet for more than two hours at a time.

You may be able to restructure a job—including the tools that support it—so that the physical limitation is no longer a barrier to performance. This type of restructuring may even accommodate people with serious physical disabilities. However, as long as a physical barrier exists, the skill to perform is blocked.

Here are some examples of *intellectual barriers* to skill development:

- A quality analyst does not have the mental bandwidth to grasp the concept of standard deviation. He has been tutored by skilled mathematicians and has read the best reference materials on the subject, but they have not helped. He is quite bright in other areas; he just has an intellectual barrier to any assignment that requires a standard deviation calculation.
- An advertising copywriter has outstanding writing skills, an impressive work ethic, and 100 percent commitment to her clients and her company's mission; however, she just does not have the creativity to generate novel ways of delivering her client's message. She has attended creativity training programs, read Edward de Bono's books, and worked with

highly creative people; however, that part of her brain just is not up to the task.

- A waiter is unable to remember anything that is not written. He works in an environment in which there is not time to write down every request ("More water," "Another fork," "Close the drapes," "Bring the check") that he hears as he passes his tables.

- A project manager has an impressively laserlike focus on accomplishing a task but cannot juggle more than one responsibility at a time. Schooling in time management, priority setting, and project management has failed to eliminate this deficiency. Since multitasking is an integral part of the job, her performance is not acceptable.

As with physical skill barriers, you should first examine the work environment to see if the deficiency is not in the individual but in the incentives, tools, technical training, or feedback. (A set of questions to diagnose the health of the work environment is presented in Figure 7.3.) You may be able to restructure the job so that it no longer requires the behavior that the individual is unable to perform. You can, through various kinds of training, attempt to develop the part of the brain that is not rising to the challenge. However, you may find that the incumbent, who probably has sufficient mental horsepower to excel in other areas, has an irremediable barrier to this responsibility.

Psychological barriers to skill requirements are complex and, to a large degree, beyond managerial purview. Examples:

- A salesperson who has all of the other requisite skills and knowledge is unable to take rejection without erupting or shutting down.
- A call center employee does not have the patience to deal with a customer who does not understand his instructions.
- A window cleaner, who generally does exemplary work, is paralyzed if asked to clean a window that is over two meters from the ground.
- An administrative assistant cannot handle the pressure of interruptions and quick-turnaround demands.
- A machine operator cannot function in an environment in which priorities are continually changing.

- A manager works in a culture in which a large amount of substantive business is done in social situations. She abhors the bar/restaurant/party/golf course environment and goes to great lengths to avoid those settings.

A number of these examples are not psychological deficiencies in clinical terms; however, they are deep-seated parts of people's psychological makeup that are serving as barriers to performance.

These examples do not directly address the illusive psychological factor known as "attitude." There is a small set of people who have a poor attitude toward everything; that aspect of their psychological structure is part of the human capability package we are discussing here. However, most people's attitude toward their jobs, their bosses, their coworkers, and their customers is less a function of embedded psychological anomalies than of the work setting influences addressed in Chapter 7.

As with physical and mental barriers, your first recourse should be to determine if the work environment or job could be restructured to deal with the psychological characteristic that is presenting a barrier to skill/knowledge development. Restructuring—which should only be undertaken if it does not compromise quality, cycle time, or cost—does not alter the characteristic of the individual's psychological constitution; however, it severs the link between that characteristic and the job requirements.

■ HOW DO PERSONAL VALUES FIT INTO THE EQUATION?

Up to now, our discussion has focused on skills and knowledge. The third leg of the human capabilities stool is *personal values and beliefs*. These tenets may be based on an individual's religious convictions, moral philosophy, code of conduct, or experience-based principles of how business should be conducted. The roots of personal values often go even deeper than psychological traits. For example:

- From its origin in the 1930s, U.S. Social Security benefits were based solely on the amount and duration of a worker's or spouse's payroll deductions. The Supplemental Security Income law enacted in 1972 granted benefits to aged, blind, and disabled citizens who did *not* qualify for Social Security benefits. Because of its network of offices and claim-processing skills, the Social Security Administration was directed to administer this program. A number of claims representatives had the skills and knowledge to process this new type of claim but would not. They believed in an earned right program but were philosophically opposed to, or did not want to work in, a "welfare" program.

- Some insurance company employees and human resource professionals are experiencing a similar task-values conflict with the same-sex partnership benefits that are now provided by a number of companies and agencies.
- A person may have religious beliefs that prevent travel, meetings, or even phone or e-mail communication on his Sabbath.
- A dedicated, highly productive worker may have a strong ethic around work-life balance. She will work hard and long, but not if it compromises her family responsibilities.
- A company may permit—and even encourage—giving gifts, tickets, and meals to foreign government officials who can facilitate business development in their countries. An international manager may refuse to engage in this practice because he believes it is wrong.
- A company may have a whatever-the-traffic-will-bear pricing policy. A sales representative's ethics may prevent her from charging more than what she believes to be a fair price for the service provided.
- An employee may have such a deep-seated preference for a certain operating style that it has become a fundamental belief. For example, an individual may be so opposed to autocratic decision making that he cannot work effectively in an environment in which that is the dominant style.

As with physical, intellectual, and psychological barriers to performance, your first recourse should be to look at the work setting. You may be able to place a skilled employee in a job or work environment that does not compromise either the values of the employee or the mission of the business. If not, there is not a match and the person will have to (and want to) go elsewhere.

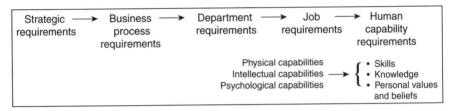

Figure 8.4 The Human Capability Factors

During strategy development (see Chapter 4), executives—usually with input from others—articulate their organization's values and beliefs. That creed forms the backbone of the norms and practices that constitute the culture of the business (see Chapter 7). When an individual's personal values conflict with the organization's values or culture, there is a human capability barrier to performance.

■ HOW DO ALL OF THESE FACTORS RELATE?

Now that we have covered all the human capability dimensions and influences, we can tie them all together. Figure 8.4 shows the relationship of all the variables.

■ WHAT ARE TYPICAL WEAKNESSES IN HUMAN CAPABILITY MANAGEMENT?

Common deficiencies in human capability management are:

- *Failing to develop a strategy* that is specific enough to guide the identification of human capability requirements.
- *Failing to design effective, streamlined processes* that facilitate the recognition of human capability needs.
- *Assuming that well-designed processes and computer systems will compensate* for human capability deficits.
- *Assuming that intelligent people ensure an adequate capability bank.* That is as illogical as saying that the most physically fit sports team is sure to win. There are different dimensions of intelligence, such as conceptual ability, creativity, analytical aptitude, memory, and street smarts. The ques-

tions: Do we have the right kinds of intelligence, deployed where they are needed? Do we fully mine that intelligence?

- *Limiting human capability identification to hard skills* (for example, engineering, accounting, sales, research) as opposed to balancing them with the equally important soft skills (for example, leadership, conflict resolution, innovation, relationship building).
- *Failing to ensure a match between personal values/beliefs and organization values/practices.*
- *Assuming that the cream will rise to the top* without training, mentoring, succession planning, and career development.
- *Overly relying on classroom training* as the vehicle for skill development. Formal training is expensive and not the most effective medium for providing or enhancing all skills.
- *When there is a performance problem, assuming that the cause lies in a human capability deficiency.*

➤ SELF-ASSESSMENT QUESTIONS

➤ *Do we have a strategy that either spells out the human capabilities we need or enables us to derive them?*

➤ *Have we identified the business process and department and job outputs required for successful implementation of our strategy?*

➤ *Have we identified the skills, knowledge, and personal values required for each job that we are examining?*

➤ *For each skill and knowledge requirement, have we identified the requisite physical capabilities, intellectual capabilities, and psychological capabilities?*

➤ *Have we identified our human capability gaps? (Where do we not have the right capabilities in the right quantity in the right place?)*

➤ *Do we have a comprehensive and current human capability plan that includes development, acquisition, and retention?*

➤ *Does the development portion of our human capability plan contain mentoring, job rotation, and other experiences that go beyond traditional training?*

■ WHAT IS THE PROCESS FOR ADDRESSING THE HUMAN CAPABILITIES VARIABLE?

The process for addressing the human capabilities dimension of your enterprise includes these steps:

1. Develop a strategy for your business, using the process outlined in Chapter 4.

    Given the profile of the executives at Customerge, the software company introduced at the beginning of this chapter, you will not be surprised to learn that they had never stopped running long enough to document their strategy. As she thought about her area of responsibility, it became clear to Sue Billingham that there is no aspect of her job—recruiting, development, compensation and benefits, culture—that does not need to be driven by the strategy.

    To meet her—and Customerge's—need for strategic clarity, she developed a simple-but-challenging set of questions to ask her colleagues on the top team. Knowing that they would not have the patience for the full process described in Chapter 4, she limited her scope to three areas of inquiry: product, market, and competitive advantage. She phrased her questions in a way that she knew would stimulate the top team's intellectual and entrepreneurial juices.

    She correctly assumed that their answers would give her the direction she needed and help them see the value in stepping up to the other strategic decisions.

    The highlight of the strategy session was the point at which the group reached consensus on Customerge's competitive advantages. In the increasingly crowded connectivity software business, they decided to bet their future on frequent upgrades and speedy technical support.

2. Identify and (re)design your strategic and key support processes, using the approach outlined in Chapter 5.

    Sue had to be particularly careful in this area. Sneaking some strategic direction setting onto the executive agenda was a lot easier than getting her colleagues to wrestle with business processes. She used the strategic decisions from

Step 1 to establish a perceived need for replicable business flows. She built her case by emphasizing these unarguable points:

➤ Customerge was no longer a handful of people around a beer-stained table at the local brasserie. The executives had to recognize that the growth of the business required the unifying hand of common approaches to core activities.

➤ Customerge was reaching the end of the honeymoon period in which sales and brand recognition growth were enough to keep its investors happy. It would soon have to generate profits, which required putting cost controls in place.

➤ Some of Customerge's most talented people were frustrated by the back-of-the-envelope way it ran its business. These people were beginning to shop their résumés.

➤ Lack of documentation lengthened the time it took to get new employees up to speed.

➤ She could not do her job without a deeper understanding of what she was hiring, training, and incenting people to do.

➤ Business processes are the way work gets done. They do not necessarily straitjacket performance. As a matter of fact, they can stimulate innovation.

➤ The executive committee was not expected to do any detailed business process work; their role was to sponsor and guide it.

Sue made the sale and quickly guided the team to the conclusion that the product development/upgrade and technical support processes were most central to Customerge's success. They designated teams to establish these processes at a high level, using an accelerated version of the methodology outlined in Chapter 5.

3. Define the outputs that each department should produce as its contribution to each key process. If you are

organized by process, department and process outputs are the same; however, if you are organized by function, key processes cross departmental lines.

During their projects, the Customerge process design teams defined departmental requirements. For example, they determined that the product development process would be world class only if Marketing had "profound knowledge" of the day-to-day work settings of its target users. So the process design includes steps in which Marketing gathers and analyzes that intelligence and uses it to identify current and potential applications of Customerge software.

4. Based on the department outputs, identify the outputs expected from individuals and/or teams. Initially, to create a manageable scope of work, you may want to limit this exercise to mission-critical positions. Do not restrict your analysis to individual contributors; leadership and managerial capabilities (see Chapter 3) may be more important to future success than those of any technical specialist.

    The Customerge process design teams identified the key jobs in each department and cascaded the departmental requirements from Step 3 into job/team requirements. For example, the call center analysts had to provide speedy, accurate, one-call answers to what Customerge called "Level One" customer inquiries.

5. Identify the (1) skills, (2) knowledge, and (3) personal values and beliefs that are required by each job output.

    Sue led the formation of small teams around each key job identified in Step 4. These teams included a member of the process design team, one or more incumbents, one or more supervisors, and, in some cases, an internal customer. The call center analyst team identified these skills, knowledge, and beliefs:

    ➤ Detailed product knowledge.
    ➤ Customer care skills.
    ➤ Oral communication skills.

➤ Questioning/listening/problem-solving skills.

➤ Problem history and customer database access skills.

➤ Understanding of the escalation process.

➤ Belief in the power of the product and in the Customerge mission.

6. Where needed to elucidate the output of Step 5, identify (a) the physical capabilities, intellectual capabilities, and psychological capabilities needed for each skill; and (b) the intellectual capabilities that are essential for each knowledge requirement.

Where it added value, the same teams identified the capabilities that underpinned the skill and knowledge requirements documented in Step 5. The call center analyst capabilities included:

➤ Able to work in a fast-paced, high-pressure environment.

➤ Able to handle angry, impatient, and often condescending callers.

➤ Able to understand heavily accented English.

➤ Bright enough to translate the customer's description of a problem into key words that enable the database to be searched.

➤ Able to sit and talk on the phone for extended periods of time.

7. Document your current capabilities in terms of the "should" established in Steps 5 and 6.

By observing, reviewing performance documents, and interviewing incumbents, supervisors, and, where possible, customers, a team of Sue's human resources people captured the current capability set for each job. They then verified their findings with line people.

8. Identify and set priorities on the gaps between your current capabilities and what you need. These gaps include:

1. Skills and knowledge that are missing (a quality gap).

2. Knowledge or skills that are possessed by too few people (a quantity gap).

3. Skill or knowledge that is not in the right places (a deployment gap). For example, your detailed product knowledge is in engineering, but not in sales. Your consumer marketing skills are in Europe, but not in North America.

In this step, you are identifying capability gaps, not performance gaps. When actual performance fails to achieve goals, there are many possible causes, only one of which is a deficiency in human capabilities.

When Customerge's actual capabilities were compared with those that were needed, the gaps were readily apparent. The highest priority gaps were call center analysts' customer relationship/communication skills, market specialists' understanding of user applications, and system architects' ability to develop business cases that support an upgrade recommendation.

9. Develop a human capability plan that describes how the gaps will be closed through:

1. *Skill development.* Classroom and on-the-job training are the most obvious vehicles for developing skills; however, they are by no means the only—and are often not the best—methods. In many cases, job aids (checklists, templates, reminders, process flows) can supplement or replace training. Computer-based performance support tools can develop skills through real-time coaching, examples, and feedback.

2. *Succession planning and career development.* Capability management is more than just ensuring that incumbents have the requisite skills and knowledge. You need a game plan for ensuring that you have capability "bench strength." Succession planning, which should be part of the repertoire of your human resources professionals, is a process for (1) identifying key managerial and nonmanagerial positions; (2) determining who should be groomed to fill those positions when they become vacant; and (3) structuring developmental experiences, such as rotational assignments, which will prepare

the people to assume those roles. Its sister process—career development—matches individual aspirations with organization capability needs.

3. *Mentoring.* Another vehicle for capability development is mentoring, in which a more senior or seasoned person guides a high-potential individual's skill development and career. Some companies have found that executive-level mentoring develops capabilities with more depth and realism than training or rotational assignments. Mentoring benefits both parties; executives use it to keep their fingers on the pulse of the organization and assess the talent in the ranks.

4. *Retention.* Star performers are always an organization's crown jewels. In a healthy economy or hot industry, they are especially rare. Training, mentoring, career pathing, and even generous compensation/equity packages do not guarantee retention of your most talented people. The strongest blocks in the retaining wall are often the cultural variables discussed in Chapter 7.

5. *Acquisition.* Internal capability development often has to be supplemented by the acquisition of talent from outside the organization. This part of the plan identifies the capabilities that are most effectively or quickly procured from outside and the recruiting and hiring process by which they will be brought in.

Sue led the development of Customerge's first human capability plan. While succession planning/career development and mentoring played a role, the cornerstones of the plan were skill development, acquisition, and retention. The highlights were:

➤ **Most of the skill development needs were not in the technical areas typically covered in Customerge's training programs.**

➤ **The plan focused heavily on addressing deficiencies in the Customerge culture, which all agreed had the greatest influence on both attracting and keeping talent.**

Given the logic of the approach that led to the conclusions and the widespread support engendered through participation in its development, Sue had no trouble selling the plan to her peers on the Executive Committee.

10. Use your measurement system (see Chapter 6) as the basis for determining which of your performance gaps are and are not being caused by human capability deficiencies.

   Sue was able to use the analysis that supported the plan to help the rest of the top team understand some of the non-capability factors that influence performance (for example, rewards, expectations, job design, and tools). She then introduced the concept of an overall performance management system. Eyes began to glaze a bit at this point, which told Sue that she had to make a stronger case. However, her colleagues were at least open to a recommendation.

11. Regularly monitor and update your human capability plan.

   The full process can be daunting. To address your immediate needs:

   ➤ Use the Self-Assessment Questions to diagnose the health of your organization's human capabilities.

   ➤ Enter the 11-step process at the step that addresses your greatest area of need. You may not need to begin at Step 1.

   ➤ Develop a plan for carrying out the other steps in the process.

All strategies and business processes require personal values and beliefs, skills, and knowledge to be deployed where and when they are needed most. These capabilities define your requirements for what is increasingly and aptly called "human capital." They take the "People are our most important asset" claim that appears on the plaque in your visitor's lobby and put some teeth and specificity into it. They give you the horsepower to make it up the steepest hills and to pass on the competitive highways. Like *leadership* and *culture*, *human capability* is a theme that runs through the other variables in the Enterprise Model.

Chapter

Leveraging Information and Knowledge

Linda Schwartz was beginning to question her decision to join TravelMate three months ago. The opportunity to be the chief information officer of the small, fast-growing luggage and travel accessory manufacturer had been appealing. She had served in second-level IT positions in large corporations and this was an opportunity to lead an organization. However, the demands from TravelMate's IT-illiterate managers were fuzzy, conflicting, and often unwise.

TravelMate has PCs in the back office. Sales representatives travel with laptops. The company has e-mail, standard word processing and presentation packages, a primitive groupware system, and a financial management suite. Not much else. Linda and her staff of two spend a large percentage of their time providing basic technical support.

During Management Committee meetings, Linda is barraged with a steady stream of questions, hot ideas, and complaints. For example:

- "Can you get us into e-commerce so we can sell internationally?"
- "Why am I unable to find out how we are doing, by product, by channel?"
- "I just heard that our Vicksburg plant has a problem that our Danville plant solved last August. How can that be?"
- "Can you link us to the point-of-sale systems in the big discount houses?"
- "Can we use computers to speed up product development?"

- "Whenever I try to find people, they are in a customer database design meeting."
- "I wish we could find some way for the Luggage Division to use some of the sales techniques that have worked so well for the Travel Accessories Division."

There is something to be said for midlevel positions in large organizations . . .

The conventional wisdom is that information technology will be the chariot that takes us to the promised land. To economists, it is the productivity engine that enables the economy to grow without inflation. To entrepreneurs and venture capitalists, it is a bottomless source of innovation and wealth. To management, it is the Holy Grail of integration, communication, learning, and—in some settings—removing the pesky and unreliable human element from the equation. And it has made centi-millionaires of the kids who used to run the high school audiovisual lab.

The information revolution has already spawned the inevitable backlash from cynics who maintain that rather than feeding paper record-keeping systems, we now are slaves to electronic files. We have replaced paper-and-leather calendar/phone directories with palm devices that are slower, less reliable, heavier, and more expensive. The paperless office is now producing more paper per capita—and more valueless paper per capita—than before the dawn of the Digital Era. The only reason we no longer have to endure boring overhead transparency presentations is because we are suffering through even more tedious computer-projected presentations. Clever graphics have replaced substance. Our bodies are riddled with radiation from our cell phones. And cashiers can no longer override a system that does not understand the bar code on the product we are attempting to purchase.

We have moved from information technology panacea to panacea. Remember when material requirements planning (MRP) and manufacturing resource planning (MRP II) were going to save those antediluvian industries that make tangible products? We are nearing the end of the era in which enterprise resource planning (ERP) systems were going to magically tie

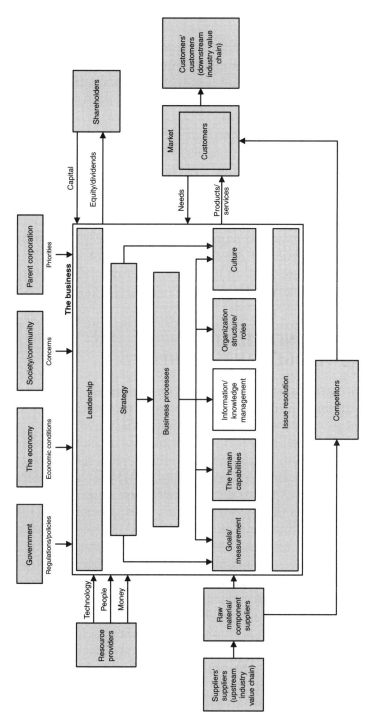

Figure 9.1 The Position of Information/Knowledge Management in the Enterprise Model

everything together. Somehow, it just never happened, or it happened at a cost that brought companies to their knees. The current electronic obsession is with customer relationship management (CRM) systems, which enable organizations to rapidly mine customer information.

The truth lies somewhere between the wild-eyed dreams of the digiterati and the dour assessments of the Luddites. Computer technology—and the Internet that it spawned—have deepened and broadened the accumulation and dissemination of information, increased the speed (if not always the clarity) of communication, and facilitated commercial transactions between customers and suppliers. On the other hand, most of the gains have been in quantity and speed, not in value. And the information revolution has yet to improve the overall quality of life for society at large.

■ WHAT IS INFORMATION/ KNOWLEDGE MANAGEMENT?

An information system is a vehicle for capturing, storing, correlating, disseminating, and/or accessing information about the external environment, internal operations, or the connection between them. While information systems can be manual, such as the tally sheets maintained by those who staff an airport information desk or the paper personnel files housed in Human Resources, most are partially or entirely computer enabled.

The quality and speed with which an organization manages its information has been an issue since the dawn of business. However, since the mid 1990s, the thinking has crystallized under the "knowledge management" banner, originally by Ikujiro Nonaka and Hirotaka Takeuchi.[1] Knowledge management (KM) is most simply defined as "getting the right information to the right people at the right time." Much of KM is getting what is in the heads of a small number of people ("tacit knowledge") available to all who can use it ("explicit knowledge"). While the KM label is unlikely to be with us forever, the need to capture, process, and appropriately disseminate information will endure. The evolution to and from knowledge is depicted in Figure 9.2.

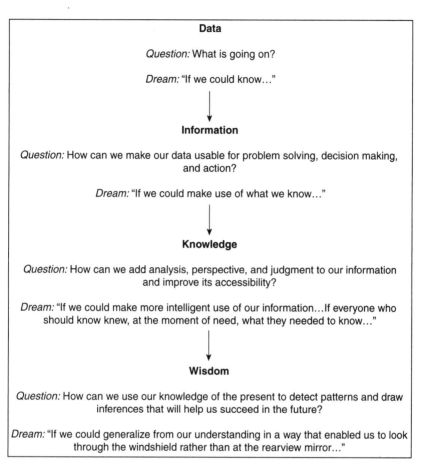

Figure 9.2 The Evolution to and from Knowledge

One of the hallmarks of a "learning organization" is its ability to tap into the knowledge that is already resident somewhere in the enterprise. The results can be dramatic. In many companies, this process is known as "internal best practice sharing." For example, Chevron saved $650 million in annual energy costs by discovering and institutionalizing a set of internal best practices. Texas Instruments generated $1.5 billion in additional annual capacity by ensuring that all 13 of its fabrication facilities emulated the processes of its highest-performance plants. Skandia leveraged its internal know-how to reduce its new venture start-up time to seven months, giving it a significant competitive advantage in an industry in which it takes an average of seven years for a start-up to reach its stride.[2]

The presence or absence of knowledge management is rooted as much in culture as in structure. A paper products manufacturer has found that its performance is considerably hampered by internal competition among its mills. The rivalry not only inhibits sharing of best practices; it even discourages sending other plants information that might facilitate problem resolution and prevention. An aerospace company has an individual hero culture that often discourages star performers from telling others what they know.

Knowledge is power. World-class organizations vest that power in the hands of the many, not the few. They do not diffuse power; they generate more of it.

However, the way in which you distribute knowledge has to be compatible with the nature of your business. For example, assemble-to-order organizations, such as Dell Computer, benefit from codification. They continuously install systems that facilitate people's access to the knowledge documented in computer or paper files. On the other hand, the strategies and cultures of organizations that provide innovative, unique solutions, such as Hewlett-Packard, base their knowledge management on personalization. They build networks that link people to the experience/ expertise in other people's heads.[3]

If your organization's knowledge is quarantined at the individual, team, department, or site level—rather than being accessible to everyone who can benefit from it—you are vulnerable.

■ WHY IS INFORMATION/KNOWLEDGE MANAGEMENT IMPORTANT?

A base level of information is the price of admission to any industry. Intelligent use of extensive information can be the foundation of a winning strategy and streamlined operations.

- A strategy is only as effective as the breadth, depth, and currency of information about trends in the external environment (see Chapter 2).

- Knowledge fuels competitive advantage. For example:

  ➤ A company may be able to beat its competitors because of its deeper understanding of a customer group. It leverages that knowledge by creating on-target new products and improving its service.

  ➤ A company's advantage may lie in its ability to rapidly introduce new products. Its strength is founded on the unimpeded flow of knowledge across its product development activities.

  ➤ A company may win through its speed of response to customer inquiries and orders. A cornerstone of that advantage is the velocity with which its people access customer history, order status, and problem resolution knowledge.

  ➤ An organization may win through its ability to secure a patent or obtain regulatory approval. It has learned how to protect that body of knowledge known as intellectual property.

  ➤ An organization's edge may lie in its ability to retain its experienced and talented people. It is caring and feeding its knowledge assets.

- *Business processes* (see Chapter 5) are only as effective and efficient as the information flowing through them.
- *Issue resolution* (see Chapter 11) is only as effective as the information that fuels problem solving and decision making.
- People's contributions are, to a large degree, a function of the information that they can access. A talented person with bad information is a substandard performer.
- Products and services cannot be created without good information. Prices cannot be established without good information. Marketing programs cannot be designed without good information. Costs cannot be controlled without good information. Quality cannot be assured without good information. Customer responsiveness cannot be exemplary without good information. Employees are frustrated if they do not have access to good information. Suppliers cannot meet your needs if they do not receive good information.

Regardless of your industry and your place in the value chain, information is nothing less than your organization's lifeblood.

■ WHAT SHOULD DRIVE INFORMATION/ KNOWLEDGE MANAGEMENT?

As depicted in Figure 9.3, *information/knowledge management* should be driven by four of the other Enterprise Model variables.

The first information driver is *strategy*. As described in Chapters 2 and 4, strategy begins by answering the following questions about the external environment:

- What are the forecasts for the economies in which we do, or might do, business?
- What are the current and future trends in our current markets?
- What are the current and future trends in markets that we do not currently serve?
- What are the competitive trends?
- What are the apparent strategies and tactics of our primary competitors?
- What technology trends could affect our business?
- What labor trends could affect our business?
- What regulatory trends could affect our business?
- What societal/community priorities and trends could affect our business?

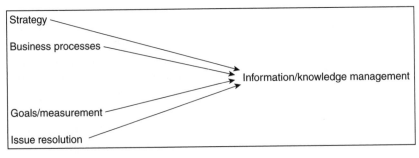

Figure 9.3 The Drivers of Information/Knowledge Management

During strategy formulation, executives use the answers to these questions as the basis for making a set of assumptions about the future. The quality of those assumptions is largely a function of the accuracy and completeness of their data and their ability to convert those data into information, that information into knowledge, and that knowledge into wisdom.

Based on this platform of information and assumptions, executives make strategic decisions that include:

- What products/services will we offer?
- What markets will we serve?
- On which products/services and markets will we place the greatest emphasis?
- What competitive advantages will enable us to win?
- How much of our growth will come from doing more of what we currently do, how much from new products/services, how much from new markets, and how much from entirely new businesses?

Once these decisions are made, executives need information that enables them to monitor performance. Through a strategic information system, executives can:

- Monitor the validity of their assumptions about the future.
- Determine whether their business is coming from the targeted products/services and markets.
- Continue to develop the knowledge dimension of their competitive advantage.
- Understand why customers are, and are not, buying.
- Understand if growth is coming from its intended sources.

The second Enterprise Model variable that should drive information is *business processes*. As discussed in Chapter 5, business processes are the flows of work through which products are developed, markets are opened, orders are filled, and people are hired. Most of what flows through business processes, even in manufacturing settings, is information.

Process needs should determine what information is gathered, when it should be gathered, the way in which it should be formatted, and where it should be sent. For example, an order fulfillment process requires speedy, accurate information on product specifications, customer history and current contacts, pricing, stock levels or manufacturing queuing, order status, delivery schedules, and invoicing. Process design should determine the role computer systems should play.

The third input to information/knowledge management systems is *goals/measurement*. You can establish viable strategic (example: market share) and operational (example: scrap rate) targets only if you have information on:

- External and internal customer expectations.
- Your organization's historic performance.
- Your competitors' performance.
- Performance information from benchmark companies outside your industry.

Once goals are established, information provides the backbone of a measurement system (see Chapter 6). A first-class information system enables you to track actual performance vis-à-vis the goals, determine trends, identify causes of deviations, and provide the information to the right people. An effective measurement system provides information that is focused, timely, accurate, and understandable. Automation can usually help achieve these objectives.

The fourth and final variable that should drive your information systems is *issue resolution*. As discussed in Chapter 11, issue resolution systems are the formal and informal ways in which concerns are identified and sorted, problems are solved and avoided, decisions are defined and made, and plans are created and implemented. Information systems:

- Bring concerns to your attention.
- Provide the foundation for issue resolution by answering questions. When did the problem start? How much would that option cost? How many person-days are available for that project?
- Capture the thinking and results from past resolutions, enabling you to draw from experience rather than starting with a clean piece of paper each time you confront an issue.

In the last few years, information systems have been widely and accurately described as "enablers." While they are critical to success and may have the biggest line item in the budget, they should be driven by—not the drivers of—strategy, processes, goals/measurement, and issue resolution.

■ WHERE DOES E-BUSINESS FIT INTO THE EQUATION?

No treatment of information is complete without a discussion of e-business.[4] E-business is the use of computer technology—hardware, software, and external and internal networks—to facilitate business transactions. It is composed of:

- E-commerce, in which products/services are sold through the Web.
- Extranets that connect an organization to, and thereby facilitate its interactions with, its customers and/or suppliers.
- Intranets, e-mail, task automation and other uses of technology that facilitate internal communication, knowledge dissemination, process effectiveness, and process efficiency.

E-business is first about business . . . then about "e." It begins with strategy. Strategically, e-business, and specifically the Internet, can

- *Change the value chain in which you do business* (see Chapter 2). For example, the Internet has made available almost unlimited information on insurance policy and automobile options and prices. That information is dramatically changing the role of insurance agents and automobile dealers. File-sharing programs have upended both the value chain and the conventional business model of the music industry.
- *Lower the entry barriers to potential competitors.* For example, a hand tool manufacturer may be able to sell directly to consumers without establishing physical locations or relying on existing retail outlets.
- *Open new markets.* Your Web site, Internet links, and Web advertising may get your message to types of buyers whom

conventional promotion never would. As soon as your Web site goes live, you are a global company (which does not mean that you have to compete everywhere). Participating in a virtual marketplace—a site that brings together buyers and sellers—may expose you to potential customers who you would not ordinarily reach.

- *Create new distribution channels.* E-commerce may serve as a vehicle for selling your products and services to those who find it easier than buying at your physical location or through your print catalog. For example, an airline can sell tickets via the Web, not simply through travel agents, the phone, and ticket counters.

Because the digital world has changed the competitive landscape and opened up avenues that were previously blocked, it puts an even greater premium on answering the strategic questions, which are, in sequence:

1. What is the future value chain in our industry?
2. What space will we occupy in that value chain?
3. How will we win in that space?
4. How can technology help us win?

Note that the technology question is fourth, not first.

The second role of e-business is to facilitate the supplier and customer interactions that are the core of an organization's primary business processes. For example:

- *Electronic Data Interchange (EDI).* Electronic links with your customers can simplify and accelerate their ordering of your products or services, your billing, and their payment.
- *Mass customization.* By digitally managing the components that go into your products, you may be able to serve a large market with products that are uniquely configured to meet individual customer needs.
- *Vendor-managed inventory.* If you are linked to your customer's point-of-sale system, you can know, within seconds, when and where one of your products has been purchased. As a result, you can serve as your customers' warehouse

and distribution infrastructure, supplying the right product, in the right quantity, to maintain their stock at the right level.

- *Increased and accelerated information access.* Customer databases enable your service representative to pull up customer histories within seconds. Problem repositories enable your help desk agent to retrieve the probable cause of and solution to a problem before a caller has to listen to more than a few seconds of '80s soft rock.

Your suppliers can provide these same services to you.

Thirdly, e-business contributes to internal operations by:

- *Increasing operating efficiencies.* You may be able to electronically create product development plans and drawings and digitally transfer them to others. Your salespeople may be able to enter orders directly into the system and transfer them to the fulfillment organization during the customer interaction. Your managers may be able to complete performance appraisal documents online, saving time and improving storage and retrieval.
- *Facilitating communication.* E-mail—fortunately and unfortunately—has enabled communication to occur easily, 24/7, across shifts, time zones, and departments. You may be able to meet electronically to make a decision that would normally require travel or a lengthy telephone or videoconference. Managers may be able to announce a change more comprehensively, consistently, and quickly than they could via paper memos, video, or meetings.
- *Increasing and accelerating information access.* Advances in data mining may enable you to readily discern buying patterns that might otherwise be invisible or take significant time to unearth. Access to uptime, materials, and maintenance information may enable you to quickly isolate the cause of a machine problem.

Not having an "e" dimension to your business is no longer an option. However, how you choose to deploy digital solutions depends on your strategy and the business processes that will implement your strategy. Regardless of the role e-business plays in your enterprise, you can derive value from creating an e-business strategy that answers these questions:

- What parts of our overall organizational strategy should be digitally enabled?
- How will we ensure that the Internet does not obsolete our place in the value chain?
- How will we protect our customer base in the digital world?
- How will e-business enable us to attract new customers?
- How will we interface electronically with our customers? our suppliers? ourselves?
- What role will our Web site play? How will the right people find it?
- How can computer technology improve the performance of our business processes?
- How can we use computer technology to improve the ways in which we manage knowledge?
- How can we use computer technology to improve our measurement?
- How can we use computer technology to improve the effectiveness and speed with which we resolve issues?
- How will we ensure that we have the systems and the technological know-how to implement this vision?
- What is the priority of each digital initiative?
- What is our plan for making all this happen?

Once you have an e-business strategy, you can determine what changes you need to make to your *culture, human capabilities,* and *structure.*

■ WHAT ARE TYPICAL INFORMATION SYSTEM WEAKNESSES?

Typical information/knowledge management weaknesses include:

- *Assuming that computers are the solution.* Computers are a means, not an end. Prematurely embracing a technology-based solution is as much of a crapshoot—and an expensive one at that—as assuming that a current problem can be resolved through a culture change initiative (see Chapter 7), training (see Chapter 8), or a reorganization (see Chapter 10). Maybe. Maybe not. Before you take any medication, diagnose the disease.

- *Putting the computer cart before the business horse.* More often than not, computers can play a major role in streamlining a business. However, "the business" has to first be defined. Without a strategy and a set of well-designed business processes, you have no way of knowing what knowledge is required for success and what role information technology should play in your operations.

  Because information technology is critically important to nearly every business and its high priests speak a language that is more arcane than other specialities ("That middleware is scalable, but does not have the bandwidth to transmit cool graphic user interface through our distributed systems."), Information Systems (IS) people are often held in awe, if not respect or admiration. Other staff functions—Human resources, Legal, and perhaps even Finance—often have to fight for a seat at the strategic table. Given the importance of a company's information backbone, it is easy to fall into the trap of allowing IS—and the systems it manages—to determine the table's size, shape, location, and construction.

  For example, enterprise resource planning (ERP) systems are designed to provide a common information platform that can be fed and accessed easily by all functions. Nobody can argue with the logic of Marketing, Sales, Operations, and Finance using common systems to access a customer history or production schedule. However, all too often, companies are expected to design their businesses to fit the requirements of ERP systems, rather than the systems being built to support an organization's strategy and processes. This is the digital tail wagging the dog.

- *Tolerating a culture that discourages knowledge sharing.* Rewarding individual heroics and fostering internal competition can inhibit knowledge management.

- *Assuming that information technology has to be managed internally.* Once you have established your strategy, you can determine the role knowledge management (KM) will play in its implementation. While you cannot outsource KM any more than you can outsource strategy formulation or culture development, you *can* outsource the mechanical aspects of information capture, storage, sorting, analysis, and retrieval. This field is more specialized than and changing faster than most. Even if KM is at the heart of your competitive advantage, you may not want to dedicate precious internal resources to keeping up with technology and its applications.

Is information technology administration one of your core competencies? If not, is it worth ongoing investment internally or is it—perhaps like pension fund administration, building maintenance, and shipping—best left to specialists?

- *Underestimating cost and time.* Research[5] has shown that only 16 percent of IT projects meet their original requirements on time and on budget. Thirty-one percent are canceled at some point during the project. The remaining 53 percent exceed their budget by an average of 89 percent and take an average of 122 percent more time than originally scheduled.

  Even if automation could help you integrate Finance and Manufacturing, monitor telephone calls, or track warranty claims, does the benefit justify the cost?

- *Installing systems that do not provide strategic information.* You have launched an initiative designed to place greater emphasis on a product or market. Nothing is more frustrating to an executive than querying the information system to see if that investment is paying off and finding that the data are not sorted in a way that enables the question to be answered. For example, you may be a business-to-business provider who has decided to target a certain size company and a certain type and level of buyer. If your information system can only give you revenue by industry and geography, it is not meeting your strategic needs.

- *Installing systems that do not provide process management information.* As discussed in Chapter 5, most core processes—business development, product development, order fulfillment, planning—cross functional lines. If Robert, the owner of the order fulfillment process, asks how much it costs to fill a large order for a certain product, the response from Finance may be "We have no idea; we can only tell you the cost of each department that contributes to order fulfillment." The fact that Robert's question cannot be answered should not suggest a reorganization; it should lead to structuring the financial information—perhaps using activity-based costing/management techniques—so that he has what he needs to manage his part of the business.

- *Assuming that having a Web site is being an e-business.* Your Web site is a pivotal ingredient, but only one ingredient, in the e-business recipe. It may not link you directly to your customers or suppliers. It does not ensure that you have the processes to deliver what it sells. It may do nothing to facilitate internal transactions.

  And having "a" Web site is not enough. It may be difficult to find. It may get your name "out there" but actually do damage because it does not position your organization in a way that reflects your strategy. It may attract customers, but not the right customers. It may generate business that you are not equipped to deliver.

- *Focusing your e-commerce initiatives solely on the front-end business processes.* Most e-commerce does not fail because of deficiencies in the customer attraction and order taking that occur at the beginning of the transaction cycle. It falls short because the back-end processes of order fulfillment and customer service are not designed to handle the business that comes in.

- *Assuming that e-business will enable you to enter new markets.* E-business can be a tool for penetrating new customer segments. However, your competitors are also looking at market expansion through e-business. If the new markets you hope to enter are international, you may find that their needs, price sensitivity, credit worthiness, and intellectual property protection laws make them unattractive.

- *Delegating information/knowledge management to the Information System Department.* Delegating knowledge management to the IS Department is like delegating people management to the HR Department or financial management to Finance. Information, like people, is a key asset and a critical component of strategy formulation and implementation. Do you want to delegate your strategy to your IS employees or consultants? IS can stoke the furnace, but executives have to drive the train.

➤ SELF-ASSESSMENT QUESTIONS

➤ *Do we have a* strategy *that clearly indicates the role knowledge will play in our competitive advantage?*

➤ *Does our strategy specify the information we need on the external environment and on our product/service and market performance?*

➤ *Do our information systems provide accurate, timely, and user-friendly strategic information?*

➤ *Does our strategy clearly indicate the role that information technology will play in our success?*

➤ *Do we have an e-business strategy, derived from our overall business strategy, that clearly establishes the role digital technology will play in our future?*

➤ *Do we have measurement systems that provide timely, accurate, and user-friendly information on how we are performing in terms of our strategic and operational goals?*

➤ *Are our* business processes *automated in the right way in the right places?*

➤ *Do our people have the skills to make the best use of computer technology?*

➤ *Do we have appropriate electronic interfaces with our customers and suppliers?*

➤ *Do we appropriately use information technology to facilitate communication and other internal interactions?*

➤ *Do our automated and manual systems capture the information we need to resolve issues effectively and efficiently?*

➤ *Do we have knowledge management systems that capture lessons-learned information (failures as well as successes)? Is this corporate memory readily accessible to those who need it?*

➤ *Does our Information Systems Department play an appropriate role—neither too central nor too peripheral—in supporting our information/knowledge management needs?*

■ WHAT IS THE PROCESS FOR ADDRESSING THE INFORMATION/KNOWLEDGE MANAGEMENT VARIABLE?

The process for designing information/knowledge management systems is

1. *Develop an overall business strategy and an e-business strategy.* Without an overall business strategy and an e-business strategy (which may or may not include e-commerce), there is no compass for information management.

   It dawned on Linda Schwartz, the overburdened CIO introduced at the beginning of this chapter, that many of the demands and complaints that descended upon her daily were rooted in TravelMate's unclear strategy. Because the management team had not stepped up to the tough choices of product definition, market definition, and competitive advantage, she had no way to identify TravelMate's strategic information needs.

   She convinced the CEO to sponsor an initial strategy session. She said that if that session were not productive, she would support pulling the plug without going any further. He agreed, tasked the finance vice president with spearheading the effort, agreed to hire an outside facilitator, and scheduled the meeting. Because of the value of the thinking, the opinion sharing, the expectations calibration, and the decision making, they ultimately held four two-day strategy sessions. With no difficulty in some cases and considerable angst in others, they answered the strategic questions that are listed in "What Should Drive Information/ Knowledge Management?" and explained in Chapter 4.

   During the third session, the executives developed an e-business strategy that answered the questions that appear in "Where Does E-Business Fit into the Equation?"

   During the fourth session, they developed a strategy implementation plan. One of the high-profile implementation teams was dedicated to information/knowledge management.

2. *Identify your strategic information needs.* These needs include (1) the external intelligence you need as a platform for strategic decision making; (2) the information that fuels your competitive advantage; and (3) the information you need to monitor the performance of your products/services, markets, and competitive advantages.

In addition to providing product development and marketing guidance, the output of TravelMate's strategy sessions enabled Linda to identify strategic information needs. Because she now understood the profiles of the target luggage users, the primary retail channels, TravelMate's future competitive advantages, and the role that e-business would play, she had direction for her development of strategic information systems.

The strategy charted her course by:

➤ Defining the price-sensitive business traveler as the primary market and profiling the customers in that market.

➤ Identifying discount retail outlets (as opposed to luggage stores, upscale department stores, or airports) as the primary distribution channel for the TravelMate brand. Household-name catalog retailers would be the primary channel for its private-labeled lines.

➤ Establishing the Internet as a primary new channel for sales and distribution. For the first time, TravelMate would sell directly to users.

➤ Specifying TravelMate's primary competitors.

➤ Committing to no-frills value (the ratio of quality—durability, size, packing space allocation, and ease of access—to price) as TravelMate's competitive advantage.

➤ Determining that the company would grow organically as opposed to searching for acquisition opportunities.

➤ Defining growth targets for the next three years.

While she and her team had a lot of work in front of them, Linda now knew the kinds of external intelligence and

TravelMate product/market performance information that systems should capture, analyze, and disseminate.

3. *Identify your business process information system needs.* These needs include (1) the information you should receive from or provide to customers and suppliers; (2) the electronic links that should facilitate the transmission of customer/supplier information; (3) the information that is needed throughout your business processes; and (4) the process steps in which automation could improve quality, reduce cost, or reduce cycle time.

Based on TravelMate's newly created strategy, the top team identified its core processes as business development, merchandising, product enhancement, and manufacturing. They chartered a team to examine improvement opportunities in each of these processes. These charters stated that the teams should (1) identify opportunities to streamline through automation, and (2) identify the lessons-learned knowledge that should be captured and made accessible.

The strategy also highlighted the high-volume customers and suppliers who would be linked electronically with TravelMate for ordering, invoicing/payment, and customer service.

4. *Identify your measurement system needs.* These needs include (1) the automated and manual ways in which you will track actual performance and compare it to goals; and (2) the automated and manual ways in which that performance information will be sorted, displayed, and provided to those who need it. See Chapter 6.

During the off-site sessions, the TravelMate executives established the strategic goals for the company. In addition to the overall sales and net income targets, the metrics included sales volume from business travelers; share of the discount chain luggage market; sales volume from Internet orders; and customer satisfaction ratings.

The strategy implementation plan included an initiative in which these strategic goals would be cascaded and measurement systems established.

The business process improvement teams formed in Step 3 were given charters that included establishing and planning for the implementation of end-of-process and upstream metrics for business development, merchandising, product enhancement, and manufacturing. These metrics will form the basis of a measurement system.

5. *Identify your issue resolution needs.* These needs include (1) the information that you should gather, electronically or manually, on an ongoing basis so that it is available for issue resolution; (2) the ways in which you will capture issue resolutions in electronic lessons-learned files; and (3) the ways in which you will ensure that this information and history are readily accessible to those who need it.

TravelMate's newly formed issue resolution system team began by identifying the information that should be available for troubleshooting manufacturing problems. Most information such as machine run rates, downtime, rework, scrap, and returns due to defects was already being gathered; however, each plant had its own system, the reliability was inconsistent, and the information was not available electronically.

They then identified the recurring decisions (for example, materials purchasing, hiring, and capital expenditure) and project plans (for example, planned maintenance, product enhancements, and safety training) that should be captured in a way that enabled them to serve as templates and information repositories.

Thirdly, they determined the circumstances under which one-time (nonrecurring) problems, decisions, and plans would be added to the database.

Lastly, they identified the need for a live-issue database for recording and monitoring the progress on unresolved issues.

All four of these actions spoke to the need for a common language in which issue resolution information and results could be readily and clearly communicated. TravelMate's executives committed to providing a universal language like the one presented in Chapter 11.

6. *Select hardware, software, and networks that will meet the needs identified in Steps 2 through 5.* This step involves decision making that places a heavy emphasis on cost-benefit analysis. These decisions should be made holistically, so that each system/database can meet a variety of strategic and operational needs. Even if enterprise systems will not do the job or will be too expensive, you want to minimize the number of hardware and software platforms and networks.

   Linda, her IS team, and a cross section of line and staff people made a series of decisions regarding architecture, hardware, software, and databases for capturing strategic information, business process information, performance measurement information, and issue information. They were pleasantly surprised at the degree to which existing systems—particularly TravelMate's underused intranet—could meet these needs.

7. *Determine how best practices will be shared across the organization.* Buckman Labs, a chemical company, uses an on-line forum as its primary knowledge-sharing vehicle. Managers monitor participation in the 54 discussion groups. Frequent users receive tangible rewards, such as trips; nonusers get an e-mail from the CEO. This approach would not fit some cultures, but it ensures that Buckman's environment supports knowledge dissemination.

   Following the decisions that were made in Step 6, Linda became worried that too much of TravelMate's knowledge management efforts would be limited to computer-generated information and seen as filling the needs of IS, rather than of line operations. She raised her concern to her colleagues on the management team. They decided that the vice president of human resources should (1) set up a process for sharing best practices across the organization and (2) identify and surface to the top team any cultural barriers to sharing this type of information. The executives realized that they had to root out anything that rewarded local information hoarding or punished documentation of mistakes from which Travel-Mate could learn.

8. *Install information/knowledge systems.* This step begins with planning and carries through implementation. It should include:

➤ Manual as well as automated information/knowledge management systems.

➤ Pilot testing where appropriate.

➤ Phased implementation where appropriate.

➤ Training where needed.

➤ A treatment of both structural variables, such as roles, and human variables, such as culture.

➤ Sound and focused application of project management and change management principles and tools.

The TravelMate Knowledge Management Team, guided by the Management Committee, developed a detailed plan for installing the systems and processes that would enable them to automate operations and manage their knowledge. The plan, which included activities phased in over a 12-month period, focused heavily on the cultural changes TravelMate needed to make.

During Step 6, it became apparent to Linda that these systems would be valuable only if they were populated with current, accurate information and accessed by those who needed it. So, one of the overriding objectives during implementation was to make data entry and access as easy as possible. Furthermore, the plan included the development and implementation of a short training program for all employees on the what/why/how of knowledge management and the use of the new systems.

An increasing percentage of the economy compiles, organizes, analyzes, and disseminates information. Intelligent enterprises convert that information to knowledge and perhaps even wisdom. While computer technology is critical to effective and efficient knowledge management, it should be driven by the needs of the business (as reflected in its strategy and processes) and deployed in ways that fit the culture. It should serve as an enterprise's engine, not as its rudder or captain.

■ NOTES

1. I. Nonaka and H. Takeuchi, *The Knowledge Creating Company: How Japanese Companies Create the Dynamics of Innovation* (Oxford: Oxford University Press, 1995).
2. C. O'Dell and C.J. Grayson, Jr., *If We Only Knew What We Know: The Transfer of Internal Knowledge and Best Practice* (Tampa: Free Press, 1998).
3. M.T. Hansen, N. Nohria, and T. Tierney, "What's Your Strategy for Managing Knowledge?" *Harvard Business Review*, March–April 1999, 106–116.
4. The core concepts in this section are derived from A. Brache and J. Webb, "The Eight Deadly Assumptions of E-Business," *Journal of Business Strategy*, May–June 2000, 13–17.
5. The Standish Group, *Chaos Study*, 1995.

Chapter

Putting Organization Structure in Its Place

Anthony Harrison, CEO of computer hardware manufacturer Giddings Technology, has to make an impact, and fast. The evidence?

- Growth has plateaued.
- Customers are complaining.
- Competitors are encroaching.
- Shareholders are selling.
- Skilled employees are leaving.
- Technology is making traditional distribution channels obsolete.

Anthony has a wide range of options.

- He can redefine Giddings' strategy.
- He can hunt for an acquisition.
- He can bring in consultants to shake things up.
- He can fill key positions with outsiders.
- He can streamline workflows.
- He can modify the compensation system.

Whether Anthony takes some—or all—of these actions, his game plan will certainly include the most common executive response to critical issues: redesigning the organization structure.

Anthony is acting in concert with conventional wisdom, which tells us that putting the right boxes on the organization chart and populating them with the right people will clarify

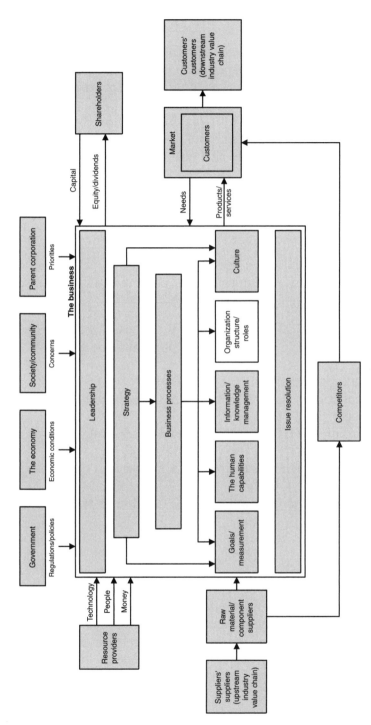

Figure 10.1 The Position of Organization Structure in the Enterprise Model

167

direction, remove barriers to exemplary performance, and improve motivation. That response is as logical as dealing with all household challenges by rearranging the furniture; it may address the need, but the odds are against it.

Assuming that reorganization is a miracle drug that cures—or at least alleviates the symptoms of—all ailments is at best naïve. At worst: beware of the side effects.

■ WHAT IS ORGANIZATION STRUCTURE?

An organization structure answers two questions:

1. Which people have been grouped together in an entity that has a shared mission and common management?
2. Who reports to whom?

Structure is typically depicted as a set of boxes, arrayed hierarchically to show the pecking order. People may be grouped:

- By function, such as Finance and Sales.
- By product line, such as Dental Care Products and Hair Care Products.
- By market, such as wholesale customers and retail customers.
- By geography, such as the Western Region and the Eastern Region.
- By business process, such as order fulfillment and product development.
- By project, such as the Eco-car Development Team and the Light Truck Marketing Program Team.

Increasingly, executives adopt structures that are hybrids of these options. In some cases, people have two or more reporting relationships. For example, Bill may officially belong to the Engineering Department (a function), but he may be working full-time on the tamper-proof packaging design initiative (a project). In this matrix structure, his solid-line boss may be the director of engineering and his dotted-line boss may be the tamper-proof packaging project manager.

In another type of matrix structure, Jean may be the director of finance for the Hampton Chemical Company's Specialty

Products Division. Her solid-line boss is the president of specialty products and her dotted-line boss is Hampton's chief financial officer.

■ WHAT ARE THE CURRENT ORGANIZATION STRUCTURE TRENDS?

The current trends in organization structure include:

- As the business environment becomes more global, organizations are *moving away from structures in which countries are autonomous fiefdoms.* For example, Dow Chemical needs legal entities in the various countries in which it operates; however, the driving force of its structure is the products that cross country boundaries.
- In a desire to increase customer focus, companies are *organizing by customer or market* rather than product or function. For example, Dell Computer has organized around its market segments: home and home office; small business; medium and large business; Internet service providers; health care; federal government; state and local government; and education.
- To break down the departmental silos that can increase cost and compromise speed, some companies are *organizing by cross-discipline business processes.* For example, a division of Motorola has established a supply management organization whose mission is to optimize that process. This organization includes people formerly located in departments such as Purchasing, Supply Quality Assurance, Reliability/Components Engineering, and Bidding/Estimating.
- To mirror the way work increasingly gets done and minimize the conflict of the two-boss matrix management structure, project-based organizations are *grouping people by project team.* Because projects, by definition, have a pinpointed beginning and end, these organizations are more fluid than other structures. Lockheed Martin, for example, is organized around its space and defense projects. People belong to project-focused organizations as opposed to being leased to projects by traditional functions like Research or Marketing. When these projects—which may last months or

years—reach completion, people are assigned to new projects. NASA has a similar structure.

- Large companies are *splitting apart businesses* that run the risk of becoming too large to be agile and entrepreneurial. For example, Microsoft does not allow the employee population in its application development businesses to grow beyond 200.

- No small firm (and very few large ones) can meet the full range of customer needs, even in a niche. As a result, many companies are establishing *strategic alliances* with firms that have complementary services. These alliances are not supplier relationships; they are partnerships of companies that each bring unique competencies to the table. Former Hewlett-Packard CEO Lew Platt said, "Once the world was simple, and so were relationships. Your partners were your allies, and your competitors were your foes. Today, people we compete with one day are our partners the next. . . . Alliances are critical. We can't do everything ourselves."[1] HP's partners include Canon, Sony, Arthur Andersen, Northern Telecom, Yokogawa, and Hitachi. Each brings a different product or service to the comprehensive solution HP offers a customer.

- To realize economies of scale and consistency, functions that are common to all businesses—Purchasing, Human Resources, Finance, Legal, Information Technology—are being grouped together in a *shared services entity* that serves as a supplier to the rest of the organization. For example, all GE companies draw on a common pool of staff services.

Each of these trends is driven by a noble goal. However, regrouping people may contribute little or nothing to the achievement of these goals. While structure is important, it is only one variable in the performance equation. And that variable is less important than most people think.

■ WHY DO EXECUTIVES GRAVITATE TOWARD REORGANIZATION?

Executives have made reorganization the solution of choice because:

- It presents highly visible evidence of their desire to change.
- They can force people to abandon their comfort zones.
- They can react to the complaints about the former structure, which—whatever it was—was unarguably imperfect.
- Unlike other improvement tactics, a reorganization can be conceived on a Monday and operational (at least on paper) on Wednesday.

A reorganization can communicate an executive's dissatisfaction with the status quo, demonstrate responsiveness, and shake people up; however, it seldom eliminates or avoids deficiencies. In and of itself, it rarely sets a business on the path to profitable growth.

■ WHAT ARE THE FALSE ASSUMPTIONS UNDERPINNING REORGANIZATIONS?

Reorganizations are typically based on two assumptions:

1. The organization structure is the vehicle through which work gets done.
2. Barriers to getting work done more effectively and efficiently lie in the organization structure.

The first assumption is always false. Work gets done through business processes such as order fulfillment, product development, complaint handling, billing, planning, and hiring (see Chapter 5). An organization structure only defines which people have been grouped together and the hierarchy of reporting relationships. It is purely an administrative mechanism.

The second assumption is frequently false. The organization structure may make it difficult for a customer question to be answered, for people to collaborate on a marketing program, or for a product to be upgraded. However, effectiveness and efficiency inhibitors are at least as likely to lie in:

- A weak strategy.
- Poorly designed business processes.

- The misuse or non-use of technology.
- Unclear or unwise policies.
- Inadequate skills.
- A dysfunctional culture.
- An incentive system that rewards the wrong performance.

A new organization design does not necessarily address any of these weaknesses.

Are reorganizations ever warranted? Certainly. However, if Andrea is an executive who wants to address her company's performance problems, she should not reorganize without evidence that a structural deficiency is among the causes. If she needs to change direction, she should not reorganize unless new groupings and reporting relationships will facilitate strategy implementation better or faster than the existing structure.

■ CAN A REORGANIZATION HURT?

Even if a reorganization does not address the underlying causes of a revenue shortfall, a failure to meet profitability targets, the defection of customers, the loss of valued employees, or the dearth of new products in the development pipeline, it dramatically symbolizes an executive's desire to get at these issues. So, can it hurt?

Yes. Reorganizations are among the most time-consuming, distracting, costly, productivity-sapping, internally focused changes that an organization can implement. The return has to justify this investment. And restructuring raises expectations. If these expectations are not met, morale and productivity can sink lower than they were before the change.

■ UNDER WHAT CIRCUMSTANCES IS A REORGANIZATION JUSTIFIED?

There are only two legitimate reasons to reorganize:

1. The current structure is impeding implementation of the organization's strategy. For example:

- Executives in a metal fabrication company decided that most of their growth would come from international customers. Their structure did not support global sales, sourcing, or distribution.

- The top team of a financial services company created a vision in which they would meet a broader set of needs in a smaller set of markets. Their product-based structure made it difficult to focus on those markets.

- The strategy of a consumer products company stated that customer service—rather than product quality or price—would be its primary competitive advantage. Service responsibilities were diffused across a number of departments, all of which had relegated service to the second tier of priorities.

2. The current structure is disrupting the flow of key business processes. For example:

- The structure in a medical products company made it difficult for Manufacturing to participate in the early stages of the product development process. As a result, new products required expensive, late-stage modifications before they could be safely and profitably produced.

- In a software company, the number of cross-functional hand-offs slowed down the order fulfillment process, causing missed deadlines and dissatisfied customers.

- The dominance of a hotel chain's geographical structure led naturally to country-specific positioning and pricing. This Balkanization impeded the company's ability to launch a marketing campaign around a universal brand identity.

Other objectives driving the desire to reorganize—clarifying roles, establishing more appropriate spans of control (the ratio of employees to supervisors), moving low-performing employees out of the way, stimulating fresh thinking—can often be accomplished through actions that entail less cost and significantly less angst.

Organization structure is simply not the most important performance variable. James, a customer service representative, has a clearly defined role that is appropriately linked to his company's strategy. He can interact easily with his external and internal customers and suppliers. He has the necessary skills and support. His measures reflect organizational priorities. He is rewarded for exemplary performance.

How critical is the name of James's department, who is sitting next to him, and whether he reports to Jennifer or Michael?

■ WHAT ARE TYPICAL ORGANIZATION STRUCTURE WEAKNESSES?

The most common organization structure deficiencies are:

- *Putting too much emphasis on structure.* As discussed above, structure is a performance variable to be addressed, but its impact is limited. A number of other Enterprise Model variables—*leadership, strategy, business processes, culture*—typically have a greater influence on performance than structure.
- *Erecting barriers.* An organization structure can present obstacles to the cross-functional flows through which work gets done. People need to be grouped together for administrative purposes; however, they should not be in fortified, impermeable silos.
- *Organizing around people rather than work.* People come and go. The structure should be designed to facilitate implementation of the strategy and deployment of the core business processes. Then, and only then, should the boxes be populated—including at the top—with the people whose talents and personalities fit the bill.
- *Sinking deep roots.* Structures need to be as pliable as strategies and business processes.
- *Creating excessive complexity.* Some structures—particularly intricate matrices in which people have multiple reporting relationships—are conceptually pure, but inefficient. If Sam's bosses have conflicting priorities or the structure makes it difficult for him to determine which departments should be involved in a decision, he is going to be held back from his optimum contribution. If your organization chart

looks like a space shuttle wiring diagram, you may have fallen into this trap.

- *Boxing people in.* You may recall the old story of the two masons who were working side by side. One of them defined his job as "laying bricks" and the other as "building a cathedral." If individuals understand the context of the structure, they are more motivated by their jobs. They can more effectively channel their efforts to "the greater good." The structure should not prevent people from interacting, innovating, challenging, and learning across organizational lines. People need an organizational home, but their contribution and growth will be stunted if they are not allowed to venture outside.
- *Permitting excessive ambiguity.* When Courtney asks for clearer direction, she is likely to be dismissed as having insufficient tolerance for ambiguity. While most professional jobs require a person to adapt to the prevailing circumstances, lack of role clarity is not a virtue. Perhaps Courtney is *appropriately* intolerant of ambiguity regarding her department's mission and the thrust of her individual contribution.
- *Ignoring personal growth.* When we are working, we live in organization structures. We all need a setting in which our administrative needs are met and in which we have the opportunity to develop our skills, influence, and stature. For example, a process-based structure may be great for the streamlined flow of product and information but may make it difficult for people to establish a career path in a specialized field. If the Finance Department is disbanded and finance specialists are sprinkled among the various processes, how do they hone their craft? With whom do they talk shop? How can they build a career in finance?

■ IS THERE A RIGHT WAY TO ORGANIZE?

Executives across industries face structural questions that include:

- Should we set up a separate e-commerce business unit?
- Should a recently acquired company be integrated or kept independent?

- Should we dedicate a group of people full-time to selling and delivering a new service?
- Should we have product managers and, if so, how much power should they wield?
- Should we have country managers and, if so, what role should they play?
- Should staff functions such as Human Resources, Information Systems, Finance, and Legal be centralized in a shared services organization?
- How many people can report to a single manager?

The answer to each of these questions is "It depends." As the examples in "What Are the Current Organization Structure Trends?" suggest, there is no universally superior structure. Nor can you insert your organization's variables into a formula that will spit out the right structure. Executives can only select the organization design that is best—which may be the current structure or one of a myriad of alternatives—by going through a multifaceted, sometimes wrenching, decision-making exercise.

■ WHAT ARE THE FACTORS THAT DETERMINE THE SUCCESS OF A NEW (OR OLD) STRUCTURE?

A team of executives has diagnosed their situation and correctly concluded that a reorganization is justified. As with other decisions that lead to major changes—a new strategy, a new computer system, a new product line, a new supplier, a move to a new location—the key to success lies in implementation. The most important success factors in organization structure implementation are:

- *Communicating* the what and why of the structure to everyone affected.
- Positioning the reorganization in the *context* of the other Enterprise Model variables that need to be addressed (rather than implying that the redesign will, by itself, cure all ills).
- Devoting more time to designing how the structure will work on the *firing line* (where the work gets done) than at the executive level.

- Developing *substrategies* for each department (each box on the organization chart) and linking those substrategies to the overall business strategy.
- Identifying the *capabilities* required by each department
- Documenting and communicating the flow of *business processes* across the departments.
- Allocating the *resources* that each department needs to fulfill its role in the business processes.
- Defining the outputs of the *key jobs* in each department and linking those outputs to the department's mission.
- Ensuring that the *performance environment* (for example, measures, incentives, and training) supports the smooth operation of the structure.
- Developing a detailed *plan* for the migration from the current structure to the future structure.
- Closely managing the *implementation* of that plan.

The last two points require underscoring and elaboration. Reorganization implementation demands the same project management rigor as a new product launch, a new market entry, or a merger. It requires breaking down the work to be done, developing milestones, assigning responsibility, allocating resources, and reporting progress. Effective structure implementation plans address the needs of both the technical system (including missions, processes, and reporting relationships) and the human system (including skills, decision-making authority, and incentives). Both of these dimensions of the plan should be underpinned by effective change management, which includes communicating features and benefits, overcoming resistance, and building commitment.

➤ **SELF-ASSESSMENT QUESTIONS**

> ➤ *Does our organization structure support the product choices, market choices, and competitive advantage described in our strategy?*
> ➤ *Does our organization structure facilitate—or at least not impede—the flow of the business processes that are most critical to the implementation of our strategy?*
> *(continued)*

(continued)

➤ *Have we avoided reorganizing except in those situations in which we have evidence that structure is the cause of performance problems or the barrier to realizing opportunities?*

➤ *When considering reorganization, do we weigh the benefits against the cost?*

➤ *Is our organization structure the result of going through a rigorous decision-making process? (See the following "What Is the Process for Addressing the Organization Structure/Roles Variable?")*

➤ *When we implement a new organization structure, do we develop a plan that addresses both the technical and the human variables?*

➤ *When we implement a new organization structure, do we employ the same project management discipline that we do in other major change efforts?*

■ WHAT IS THE PROCESS FOR ADDRESSING THE ORGANIZATION STRUCTURE/ROLES VARIABLE?

Executives and managers should take the following steps on the path toward or away from reorganization:

1. *Evaluate and, if necessary, refine the business strategy.* Strategy should drive structure. As discussed in Chapter 4, strategy should provide fact-based, clear, compelling, boundary-setting answers to these questions: What products/services will we offer and not offer? Which products/services will we emphasize? What markets will we and will we not serve? Which markets will we emphasize? What competitive advantage(s) will cause us to be successful? How will we measure our strategic performance?

   Anthony, the Giddings Technology CEO referenced in this chapter's opening paragraph, and his top team decided that they would offer a wide variety of computing appliances

(servers, desktops, laptops, palmtops), but would not offer software or peripherals such as printers, scanners, and modems. They decided to target the corporate, as opposed to the consumer, market. They committed to winning based on custom features, speed of delivery, and ease of use. They assessed their performance in terms of revenue growth, profitability, repeat business, customer satisfaction ratings, and share of the corporate market.

2. *Identify the business processes that are most critical to the successful implementation of the strategy.* Strategy and business processes should be the two primary drivers of structure. As discussed in Chapter 5, business processes—the activity flows through which work gets done—must be supported by the structure.

Giddings' executives identified their core processes as:

➤ Customer-need identification.

➤ Product customization.

➤ Order fulfillment (for the traditional and e-commerce dimensions of their business).

➤ Technical support.

Other "customer touch" processes such as marketing, pricing, and billing, and internal processes such as hiring, planning, and financial reporting, are operationally important but not as strategically critical to Giddings' success.

3. *Define the characteristics of an organization structure that supports the strategy and the core processes.* To ensure that the structure evaluation is comprehensive and that there is a framework for the debate, it is best to begin by developing a set of decision criteria, or objectives. These objectives enable you to compare strengths and weaknesses as you decide among alternative structures. In some cases, they are more effectively used as the specifications for your *design* of the best structure.

As part of their strategy implementation planning, Giddings' executives determined that their organization structure should enable them to:

➤ Focus on the three top-priority products and two top-priority corporate markets.

➤ Quickly and accurately identify customer needs.

➤ Configure solutions to meet these needs.

➤ Minimize the time it takes to fill an order accurately.

➤ Minimize the time it takes to resolve customer technical problems.

4. *Define other objectives to be met by the organization structure.* In addition to supporting your strategy and core processes, you want your organization structure to serve other purposes. Your additional objectives may relate to administrative, cost, and people needs. In some cases, these selection criteria carry nearly as much weight as those related to strategy or business processes.

Anthony and his team determined that their structure should:

➤ Motivate employees.

➤ Maximize role clarity.

➤ Minimize cost.

➤ Establish a manageable employee-to-supervisor ratio.

➤ Support career development.

➤ Minimize implementation time.

➤ Minimize disruption during implementation.

5. *Generate alternative organization designs.* In this step, the options are described at a level of detail that enables them to be assessed against the decision criteria and compared to other options.

Giddings' executive team concluded that they could organize:

➤ By product (a server division, a desktop division, and a laptop/palmtop division).

➤ By market (a large business division, a small business division, and a government division).

➤ By geography (Europe, Asia/Pacific, and the Americas).

➤ By function (for example, Manufacturing, Research and Development, and Sales).

➤ By process (for example, product development, order fulfillment, and customer care).

➤ By project (for example, the Asian Expansion Team, the Server Commercialization Team, the Enterprise Resource Planning System Installation Team).

➤ Around a hybrid in which product is the primary sort and projects are the next cut (for example, the WP235 Upgrade Team within the Palmtop Division).

The current functional structure, with some enhancements, was one of the alternatives that the Giddings executives evaluated. Imperfect as it was, they were open to the possibility that it was as good as or better than the other candidates.

They were able to reject some of the options—such as "by geography" and "by project"—without serious consideration.

At a corporate level, a company with businesses that do not share a product/service or market (for example, GE's appliance, jet engine, and financing businesses) can organize by business unit. However, each business unit needs to adopt one of the structures listed above.

6. *Select the best organization structure.* Since there is no universally correct structure, the purpose of Step 6 is to determine the organization design that is best for the unique needs of a business at a point in time. This step surfaces both the strengths and the weaknesses of each alternative structure. Shortcomings in the strongest candidates may be minimized or eliminated by modifying the design to incorporate aspects of other alternatives.

Giddings' top team:

➤ Assessed the relative importance of each of the selection criteria that were developed in Steps 3 and 4.

➤ Used those criteria to systematically assess the relative strength of each of the alternatives identified in Step 5 (and the new hybrid alternatives that emerged).

➤ Determined which alternative best met the entire set of criteria.

➤ Assessed the risk of the two strongest alternatives.

➤ Made their choice.

They ultimately decided on a market-based structure. To retain product focus and expertise, they housed a set of product managers in a central marketing function.

The decision making was not painless. However, the executives concluded that the consequences of the structure decision demanded that they invest the time to thoroughly and creatively go through this process.

7. *Develop and carry out a structure implementation plan.* Using the guidelines cited under "What Are the Factors That Determine the Success of a New (or Old) Structure?", develop an implementation plan. That plan should cover the waterfront of technical and human factors, interface with other projects and the other variables in the Enterprise Model, and be carried out at an appropriate pace. A key element in the plan should be the definition of roles (outputs and standards) at all levels. Then, use project management and change management principles to steer it to success.

Steps 3 through 6 require sound decision making. Step 7 requires strong project management. Methods for decision making and project management are outlined in Chapter 11.

A new strategy may suggest a new organization structure. A reorganization may help streamline business processes, serve as a powerful symbol of the evolution to a new culture, or enable talent to blossom. However, while many of the costs of a reorganization are hidden, your total investment could easily be as great as that required by the development and launch of a new product or marketing campaign. And it may not resolve the issues that served as your initial call to arms. When considering a reorganization:

- Specifically define the issues (current problems, potential problems, opportunities) that are facing your business.
- Determine the degree to which structure, as opposed to other variables in the Enterprise Model, is causing the problems or could facilitate the realization of the opportunities.
- Go through the strategy/business process-driven steps outlined above to determine whether an alternative structure would be superior to your current structure and whether it is worth the cost of implementation.
- Define department, team, and individual roles that enable the structure to take root.

Organization structure is important. It is where people live. However, it is purely a support system for the other variables. As such, it should be considered only after most of the other Enterprise Model variables have been addressed.

■ NOTE

1. *Industry Week*, 19 December 1994, p. 30.

Chapter

11

Resolving Business Issues

Paula Weichert has a problem with problems. The president of Baltimore Holdings, Inc. (BHI), a distributor of fresh and packaged foods to the nutrition store market, is proud of the company's record of 120 consecutive quarters of record sales and profit. BHI's strategy and operations appear to be on track. Its people are among the most capable in the industry.

However, as in every company, problems crop up. Suppliers occasionally miss deadlines, causing BHI to miss its delivery commitments or incur additional shipping costs. Last week, labels were falling off canned products. A couple of months ago, a large number of customers received short shipments.

There is no evidence that BHI's problems are bigger than those at other companies. Paula's frustration is based on the fact that the company continually confronts problems it has faced before. Last year's problem is back again. Problems that have been solved in one distribution center are re-solved in another center. Even that situation would be tolerable if the problems were eliminated quickly. However, whenever a problem surfaces, the normally streamlined organization goes into panic mode. Task forces are formed, people are dispatched to collect every conceivable piece of data, and departments spend valuable time building cases for their innocence.

Decision making is also inefficient. Whenever a piece of capital equipment is to be purchased, a product choice made, or a marketing program selected, BHI's productivity suffers. Staff people produce position papers the size of the Manhattan telephone directory. Managers spend days in meetings that have been compared to communal root canals. People who normally work well together form warring factions. Just when consensus appears to be forming, a new option or risk or opinion brings them back to square one. In Paula's opinion, the decisions that emerge from all of this activity are no better than they would be if a brave individual just made a from-the-hip choice.

Special projects are just as painful. They take people away from normal duties for inordinate amounts of time, always take longer than expected, and consume cash at alarming rates.

Paula cannot believe that every organization has this weakness. However, she does not know where to start.

Paula's situation is not unique. Perhaps your organization is characterized by:

- Steady, profitable growth.
- A robust, investor-captivating stock price.
- Dynamic, visionary leadership.
- A viable, well-implemented strategy.
- Clear, challenging-but-attainable goals.
- Effective, streamlined business processes.
- Talented, skilled people.
- A motivating, strategy-supporting culture.
- State-of-the-art, knowledge-enhancing information systems.
- A clean, process-buttressing organization structure.

If this describes your situation, you may want to make sure that you are awake and not under the influence of controlled substances. If so, can you indefinitely hang the "Gone fishing" sign on your office door? No. An American president with a healthy economy, no soldiers engaged in war, and a 75 percent approval rating can be brought to earth by the realization that there is still this place called the Middle East. British prime ministers will always have Ireland. DuPont will always have Greenpeace. Civilization will always have television. Similarly, executives and managers will never work themselves out of a job; they will always have issues.

Just as *leadership* and *culture* are woven into the fabric of the entire Enterprise Model, *issue resolution* is a necessary support

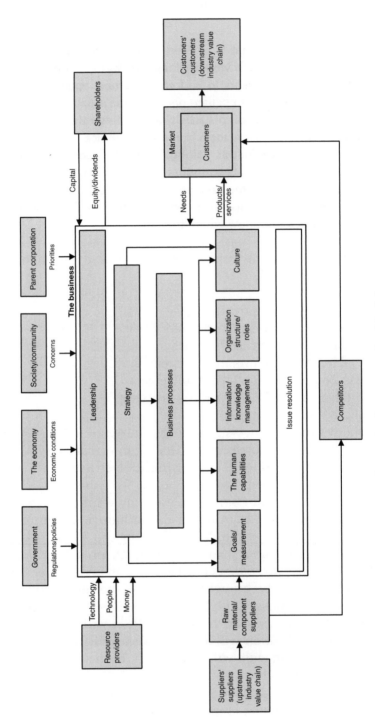

Figure 11.1 The Position of Issue Resolution in the Enterprise Model

system for all the other variables. Weaknesses in the design and execution of *business processes* or *organization structure,* for example, can be no more than speed bumps in an organization with exemplary issue resolution capability. Since issues are bacteria that can never be completely eradicated (and some types of which are beneficial), one could argue that superior issue resolution is the most universally formidable and sustainable competitive advantage.

■ WHAT IS AN ISSUE?

An issue is a nonroutine stimulus that requires a response. It is nonroutine because it does not occur as part of the normal package of inputs that arrive each day. It may be a threat, an opportunity, or both. Its genesis may be outside or inside the organization. It may be large or small. It may be simple or complex. It may be obvious or subtle. It may confront an entire enterprise, a department, a business process, a team, or an individual. It may be facing you today or looming in the future. It may be recurring or unprecedented.

■ WHAT ARE THE DIFFERENT TYPES OF ISSUES AND THE PROCESS FOR ADDRESSING EACH?

While issues come in an infinite number of shapes and sizes, they represent a limited number of species. Each of the following sections describes one of the seven types of issues and outlines a process for addressing it.

Issue Type One: Where Are We Going?

In this type of issue, your organization's direction is unclear, questionable, or not viable. For example, you have not decided whether you should pursue the Internet as a sales and distribution channel. You have been targeting a market that has yet to respond and you are beginning to wonder if it ever will. Your historical competitive advantage has eroded. You have an acquisition opportunity and are not sure whether to pursue it. These are *strategic* issues.

Addressing Issue Type One: Setting Direction

The process for addressing this type of issue—*strategy formulation*—is described in Chapter 4.

Issue Type Two: Why Did This Happen?

In Type Two issues, you need to discover the reason something is occurring. Type Two issues come in two forms:

- *Performance is failing to meet expectations, the cause is unknown, and knowing the cause is important.* You are confronting an undesirable occurrence or situation. The fix depends on the cause. For example:

  ➤ You are losing customers. The organization is rife with different explanations. Your executive team members do not want to take action until they are sure they understand the reason(s) for the defections.

  ➤ Europe is not meeting its sales forecast and your vice president of sales wants to find out why.

  ➤ Project managers are failing to submit complete project status reports and the project sponsors want to know why.

  ➤ Travelers delay billing by submitting their expense reports late and your head of accounts payable wants to know why.

  ➤ A machine's output has decreased and the machine operator wants to know why.

  As these examples illustrate, people at all levels have Type Two issues.

- *Performance is surpassing expectations, you do not know why, and it is important that you understand the cause.* In this situation, the news is good; however, if you understand the cause of the positive situation, you may be able to sustain the strong performance, migrate it to other areas, or improve it even more. For example:

➤ Market share has increased steadily in the last year and your executives want to understand why.

➤ Cash flow has increased during the past quarter and your comptroller needs to know why.

➤ You are beginning to attract higher-caliber job applicants and human resources wants to know why.

➤ A weak sales representative's revenue production has just increased and the director of the Western Region needs to know why.

➤ The demand for your product in France has skyrocketed and the people in International want to understand why.

Addressing Issue Type Two: Finding Cause

A process for addressing Type Two issues is *Problem Analysis*[1]

1. *Describe the problem* by answering:

   ➤ What should be happening? What actually is happening? What similar problems could be occurring, but are not?

   ➤ Where is the problem appearing? Where—if anywhere—is the problem not appearing?

   ➤ When did the problem first occur? When has it occurred since? When—if ever—has the problem not occurred?

   ➤ How big and widespread is the problem? How big could it be?

2. *Identify possible causes* by answering:

   ➤ What is different about the types of problems that are occurring and those that are not? The locations in which the problem appears and those in which it does not? The time at which the problem started and the period before that? The time(s) at which the problem occurs and the time(s) at which it does not?

➤ If this problem has not been around forever, what has changed?

➤ How could the changes have caused the problem?

➤ If the problem has been around forever, how could the differences between the problem and nonproblem areas be the crux of the cause?

3. *Evaluate possible causes* by answering:

➤ How does each possible cause explain the information in the problem description?

4. *Confirm the true cause* by answering:

➤ How can we test our most probable cause in the real world to verify that it is the true cause?

If you are searching for the reason for an uptick in performance or an explanation for performance that has been exemplary from day one, these questions still apply. All you need to do is replace "problem" with "desired performance."

If your problem involves people (for example, sales representatives selling smaller projects, analysts turning in reports with errors, managers failing to deal with poor performers) you may want to go beyond laserlike cause-effect analysis. Just as a single ailment may stimulate you to schedule a complete physical examination, you may want to conduct a systemwide analysis of the variables in the work setting.

A process for conducting this diagnosis is "Performance System Analysis,"[2] which includes these questions:

- Are the job expectations and priorities clear and reasonable?
- Do people have the information and tools they need to do a good job?
- Are business processes and jobs designed in a way that supports optimum performance?
- Do people have the skills and knowledge to do the job?
- Do people have the physical, mental, and psychological capacity to do the job?
- Are people rewarded, or at least not punished, for doing a good job?

- Do people get regular, specific, constructive feedback on their performance?

These Performance System Analysis questions can also be asked when performance has improved or is surpassing expectations (for example, engagement profitability has gone up, more projects are meeting schedule, costs have gone down, Region Three consistently outperforms the other regions). In these situations, you would like to understand the factors—in the people and/or in their work environment—that are supporting the strong performance. If performance is not exemplary everywhere, these questions help tease out differences. If it has not been exemplary since the doors opened, they help identify relevant changes.

Issue Type Three: Which Way Should We Go?

A Type Three issue is simply a situation in which you have at least two options and want to pick the one that has the greatest odds of success. The focal question for this type of issue is "Which one is best?" Type Three issues come in three forms:

- *You know the cause of a problem or the cause does not matter. You need to decide how to respond.* For example:

   > Your latest product release has bombed in the market and your research clearly indicates that the reason is that the product is overly feature heavy and confusing to users. You need to decide among options that include scrapping the product, repositioning the product, and retooling the product.

   > You are losing talented employees to another industry and you know that the reason is that they are being offered equity. You need to decide whether to offer equity, install a profit-sharing plan, increase salaries, create a more appealing culture, and/or pursue one or more of the many other employee retention alternatives.

   > Your margins have decreased and your Problem Analysis indicates that the erosion is due to an

increase in the price of raw material. You need to decide whether to increase your prices, find a new supplier, negotiate a more favorable contract with your current supplier, or use another material.

➤ You know that managers are failing to develop career plans for employees because they find the paperwork burdensome. You need to decide whether to cut some of the administrivia out of the current process, put incentives in place for completing the plans, design an entirely new process, and/or have human resources do more of the work.

■ *You know why performance has improved or a positive development has occurred, or the cause does not matter. You now need to decide how to respond.* For example:

➤ A customer has just expanded its operations and thereby increased its need for your services.

➤ A key competitor has just declared bankruptcy.

➤ You have sold more long-term contracts. Because you have longer lead times, you could use slower, less-expensive shipping methods.

➤ Interest rates have just come down.

■ *You are not facing a problem, a performance improvement, or new development. You simply have to make a choice.* For example:

➤ Executives have to decide the amount of next quarter's shareholder dividend and whether to set up an operation in another country.

➤ Engineers must decide which product features to recommend and how they can cut costs out of the manufacturing process.

➤ An administrative assistant has to decide how to schedule that day's work and how to route the boss from Cleveland to Katmandu.

➤ A technical support manager has to hire 40 call center employees from among 275 applicants.

Addressing Issue Type Three: Making a Choice

A process for addressing Type Three issues is *Decision Analysis:*

1. *Clarify the purpose of the decision* by answering:
    - ➤ Why are we making this decision?
    - ➤ What is the scope of the decision? (Are we buying a car or selecting a mode of transportation to work?)
2. *Evaluate alternatives* by answering:
    - ➤ What are the objectives (selection criteria) that will help us assess the strengths of each alternative (option)?
    - ➤ What is the priority of each of the objectives?
    - ➤ What are the alternatives?
    - ➤ In terms of each objective, how does each alternative fare against each of the other alternatives?
3. *Assess risks* by answering:
    - ➤ What could go wrong if we select this alternative?
    - ➤ How likely and damaging is each risk?
4. *Make the decision* by answering:
    - ➤ Which alternative strikes the best balance between strengths (meeting our objectives) and risks?

This decision-making process can be the framework of a brief hallway conversation or a detailed, formal report in which objectives are numerically weighted, alternatives are scored, and the probability and seriousness of risks are rigorously assessed. It can be used by an individual or a team. It can—and should—strike a balance between analytical thinking and creative thinking.

Issue Type Four: How Do We Get There?

In a Type Four issue, your challenge is to successfully implement a decision. Your need to take action does not fit the conventional definition of "issue." However, because many good decisions never bear fruit due to poor execution, this type of need should be elevated to issue status. There are two calls to action:

- *You or someone else has decided how to respond to a* problem. *It is time to act.* For example:

  ➤ You have to institute the safety procedures that will eliminate the violations that put you out of regulatory compliance.

  ➤ You have to successfully launch the marketing program that has been designed to restore your market share.

  ➤ You have to outsource your information technology function, which the top team thinks is the best way to improve the quality and reduce the cost of systems support.

  ➤ You have to streamline your cumbersome product development process, which is universally seen as the barrier to speedier time-to-market.

- *You or someone else has created or decided how to respond to an* opportunity. *It is time to act.* For example:

  ➤ A key customer has just offered you "preferred supplier" status. You need to lead the organization through the certification process.

  ➤ Your executive team has decided to forge an alliance with a firm that has complementary services. You are responsible for establishing that partnership.

  ➤ Your plant management team has decided on the next generation of machinery. You need to manage its purchase and installation.

  ➤ You have received a large order and are responsible for delivering it on time.

Addressing Issue Type Four: Planning and Taking Action

Decision making is the easy part; execution separates the adults from the children. If the implementation challenge is complex, it is typically called a "project" or an "initiative." A process for addressing this situation is *Project Management.*[3]

1. *Define the project* by answering:

> ➤ What is the purpose of this project?
> ➤ What results will this project achieve? Within what constraints must it operate?
> ➤ How will we break down the work into manageable activities?
> ➤ What resources (human, financial, equipment, facilities) are required?

2. *Plan the project* by answering:

> ➤ Who will be responsible for each part of the project?
> ➤ In what order must the activities be carried out?
> ➤ How much time must be devoted to each activity? What are the start and stop times of each activity?
> ➤ How will we ensure that the right resources, in the right quantity, are scheduled at the right time?
> ➤ How will we protect the plan from those things that could go wrong? (See "Issue Type Five.")

3. *Implement the project* by answering:

> ➤ How will the project be kicked off?
> ➤ How is the project progressing against the plan?
> ➤ What midcourse modifications do we need to make?
> ➤ How will the project be officially closed out? How will we make sure we learn lessons from this project?

Some implementation requirements are not full-fledged projects; they are "just do its." They don't demand an answer to all the questions listed above. For example, a lawyer has to file a brief. An installer has to set up a workstation. A construction foreman has to button up a worksite before an impending storm. While the essence of the define/plan/implement process outlined above is a valuable mental discipline in all implementation situations, "just do its" may involve only one person for a couple of hours and not require anything in writing. However, actions of all magnitudes deserve at least a brief consideration of potential problems and opportunities, which are covered in the next two sections.

Entrepreneurs and other species of optimists say that there are no problems, only opportunities. While it is difficult to see the loss of a customer, a product liability lawsuit, or a downturn in sales as an opportunity, many situations do have both a problem and an opportunity dimension. For example:

- A slide in stock price is an opportunity to buy back shares.
- The loss of three finance people may present an opportunity to replace them with people who have different skills.
- A falloff in customer satisfaction ratings may stimulate the repair of processes that have been broken for a long time.
- A formidable new competitor may force executives to focus their strategy and strengthen their operations.

In all cases, you need to determine whether a cause needs to be found (Type Two), a decision needs to be made (Type Three), or an action needs to be taken (Type Four).

Issue Type Five: How Can We Avoid Serious Problems?

In Type Five issues, you may be insulating a plan that you have developed using the Project Management process described above. Or you may be taking a "just do it" action that does not warrant a detailed plan. In both cases, you want to address potential problems that are worthy of your attention today because they have a high probability of occurring and, if they do rear their ugly heads, will cause significant damage. For example:

- Your prizewinning researcher is vulnerable to overtures from the competition.
- The economy in one of your target countries is likely to weaken.
- An executive wants to minimize the fallout from her termination of a senior person.
- An information system specialist wants the next upgrade to go smoothly.
- A field service technician wants his fix to be permanent.

Addressing Issue Type Five: Minimizing Future Trouble

A process for addressing Type Five issues is *Potential Problem Analysis:*

1. *Identify potential problems* by answering:

    ➤ What could go wrong?

2. *Identify likely causes* by answering:

    ➤ What could cause each potential problem to go wrong?

3. *Take preventive actions* by answering:

    ➤ What can we do to reduce the odds of each potential problem occurring?

4. *Plan contingent actions* by answering:

    ➤ What can we have ready to minimize the damage if it goes wrong?

    ➤ What will trigger the contingent actions as soon as possible after the problem has occurred?

There are different levels of preventive action. For example, there may be a number of ways that you can minimize the odds of losing your world-class researcher. If she signs a lucrative long-term contract, you can be pretty sure that you will have her on board for that period of time. If that is not possible, you may take actions that do not eliminate the possibility of the problem, but lower the odds that it will occur. You may provide additional research funding, involve her in the restructuring of her work environment, remove administrative tasks, and/or provide a research assistant.

In some cases, you may take a number of actions to minimize the chance that the problem will occur. For example, you may choose to address the potential problem of a lost-time accident by providing safety training, improving safety signage, holding weekly safety meetings, and designating a safety captain in each zone of the plant.

Alas, there are some situations in which you have little or no ability to avoid a problem. You may have limited influence on the economy, a piece of environmental legislation, or a change in your supplier's strategy.

You may not be able to take any preventive action or your preventive actions may fail. So, you should develop contingent actions that minimize the damage caused by a potential problem that finds its way to your door. For example, you will take a number of actions to prevent the departure of your talented researcher. If those actions are unsuccessful, you want to be ready. Your contingent actions include developing a process for filling her position, establishing contacts in the research community who can serve as a candidate-search network, and identifying a headhunter who specializes in this area.

You have taken actions to prevent accidents. However, a mishap—or even a disaster—can occur. So you will plan contingent actions: ensuring that fire extinguishers, spill containment equipment, and medical supplies are available in every section of your facility; training personnel in the use of the equipment and in basic first aid techniques; and securing the right kinds of insurance with the right levels of coverage.

There are limits to the number of preventive and contingent actions you can take. There are trade-offs between the benefits and cost of each action. To facilitate your choice of the action(s) you will take, you can use the Decision Analysis process outlined in "Addressing Issue Type Three."

Issue Type Six:
How Can We Take Advantage of an Opportunity?

Issue Type Six is the flip side of Type Five. Just as you searched for and took actions to address potential problems that could impede your action, you want to identify and address opportunities that could enable your action to surpass expectations.

In some cases, you may have had no reason to expect some of the opportunities. For example, your building maintenance customers may have a dramatic, unforeseen increase in demand for your services.

In other cases, the opportunity may be an additional benefit from an action that you are already planning to take. For example, you are in the toy business and are launching a marketing campaign directed at your retail channel. There are two potential opportunities: (1) the response from the retail stores could far exceed even your most optimistic projections and (2) the campaign could generate a positive reaction from outside its target audience—your wholesale distributors.

To examine the "glass half full" aspect of three of the examples from Issue Type Five:

- The executive takes a broader look at the opportunities that could come with the replacement of the dismissed employee.
- The information system specialist thinks about additional objectives that could be achieved during the upgrade.
- The field service technician identifies the additional benefits that could be reaped during the repair call.

Addressing Issue Type Six: Maximizing Future Benefits

A process for addressing this type of issue is *Potential Opportunity Analysis:*

1. *Identify potential opportunities* by answering:

   ➤ What could go better than expected?

2. *Identify likely causes* by answering:

   ➤ What could cause each potential opportunity to occur?

3. *Take promoting actions* by answering:

   ➤ What can we do to maximize the probability that the opportunity will present itself?

4. *Plan capitalizing actions* by answering:

   ➤ What can we do to maximize the benefits from the opportunity?

   ➤ What will trigger our capitalizing actions as soon as possible after the opportunity has presented itself?

You take promoting actions because you do not want to merely sit back, cross your fingers, and hope. You want to position your door so that opportunity is more likely to knock. Let us pick up the toy example presented above. Without defocusing on the retail channel, you may want to include wholesalers in the target audience for your marketing program. Or you may want to explore ways of developing a marketing approach that pushes the right buttons in both the retail and wholesale channels. Or you might structure the marketing program so that the retailers respond to the wholesalers rather than directly to you.

The need to plan capitalizing actions is illustrated by an effective television advertisement for a U.S. shipping company. An upstart Internet company goes online. A group of principals crowds around a computer screen as one of them pushes the button to activate their Web site. When their first order comes in, they cheer. Then 10 orders come in. Then, still within the first few minutes, a hundred. They are ecstatic. As a thousand orders come in and then 10 thousand, their faces fall. The clear message: They were not prepared for this volume of response. The question: Having built a door and placed it where opportunity can not miss it, how are you going to make sure that someone is home when it knocks?

For example, if the retailer or wholesaler response to your toy marketing program exceeds your expectations, you want to have enough products. If you do not want to risk sitting on a mountain of inventory, perhaps you can arrange for your suppliers and manufacturing people to run a third shift as soon as there is a clear indication that the volume is going to exceed projections. You may want to have temporary staff identified for the increase in shipping requirements. You may want to have Finance develop an accelerated invoicing process.

As with preventive and contingent actions, the selection of promoting and capitalizing actions can be aided by Decision Analysis.

If you are managing a project that is complex enough to warrant a written plan, both Potential Problem Analysis and Potential Opportunity Analysis should be built into its steps.

Issue Type Seven: How Can We Find Our Way through This Thicket?

In Issue Type Seven, you have a muddy or complex situation that does not fit neatly into any of the categories described above. Unlike the other six types, your objective is not to resolve or analyze an issue, but to understand it, put it into the context of the other issues you are facing, and plan for its resolution.

It is not unusual to hear executives bemoan their organization's "customer satisfaction problem" or "product launch issue" or "e-business challenge" or "morale decline" or "cost concern." These "issue baskets" require clarification and dissection before they are actionable.

For example, perhaps your "customer satisfaction problem" can be pinpointed as "The results of the last customer survey show a decline in three key categories." Now, you can ask if you know the reason(s) for the decline. If not, it is a cause-unknown problem (Type Two); if so, it is a cause-known problem that requires a corrective action decision (Type Three). If you already know what to do about it, your next step is to take action (Type Four).

Perhaps your "product launch issue" cannot be pinpointed because it is a melange of problems, decisions, and actions, including:

- A cause-unknown problem: the unwarranted time it takes to launch a new product.
- A cause-known problem in which a decision needs to be made: the excessive cost of prototype development.
- An action to be taken: implementing the new product development funding approval policies.
- Potential problems and potential opportunities associated with the upcoming launch of the F432 product.

These different species of issue cannot be addressed while they are bundled.

Addressing Issue Type Seven: Clarifying and Planning to Resolve Concerns

An executive has a "Wall Street concern." A plant manager has a "supplier issue." A branch bank manager has a "loan problem." A project manager has just inherited a complex initiative. A process for addressing their immediate needs is *Situation Appraisal:*

1. *Identify and clarify concerns* by answering:

    ➤ What are our current and future threats and opportunities?

➤ What evidence do we have that each of these concerns needs attention?

➤ Which concerns need to be separated into their component parts before they can be resolved? What are those component parts?

2. *Set priority* by answering:

➤ What is the relative priority of our concerns based on the seriousness, urgency, and growth of each?

3. *Plan next steps* by answering:

➤ Which of the issue types does each concern represent and, as a result, which type of analysis or action is required?

4. *Plan involvement* by answering:

➤ Who owns the issue and any subissues?

➤ Who should be involved in the resolution of each issue?

This last question is important enough to warrant its own section.

■ WHO SHOULD BE INVOLVED IN ISSUE RESOLUTION?

The processes outlined above indicate "what" and "how," but not "who." Should these tools be used by individuals, small groups, or large groups? If a group is to use a process, should it be in a meeting setting? If so, what type of meeting?

There are five different levels of involvement:[4]

- The person responsible for resolving the issue (the "leader") resolves it alone.
- The leader involves others, one-on-one, purely as information sources.
- The leader involves others, one-on-one, both as information sources and as providers of advice and counsel.

- The leader convenes a meeting. All parties contribute information, analysis, and opinions. People talk to each other, not just to the leader. The leader makes the decision.
- The leader convenes a meeting. All parties contribute information, analysis, and opinions. The leader sets boundaries, but relinquishes the right to make the final decision. The decision is made by consensus.

In the abstract, all five of these participation modes are equally viable. Rather than adopting one of them as a consistent operating style, talented leaders employ the level of involvement demanded by the issue. The questions that lead them to one of the five alternatives are:

- Whose information and thinking do I need to reach a quality resolution?
- Who needs to participate because (1) their commitment is critical to successful implementation and (2) they are unlikely to commit if they do not participate?
- Whose decision-making skills need to be developed?
- If put in a group setting, can the others be expected to perform intelligently, efficiently, and in the best interests of the company?
- What are the consequences of me making this decision? What are the consequences of the group making the decision?
- How much time do I have?

Simply asking these questions, which takes no more than two minutes, can help a leader improve the effectiveness and efficiency of issue resolution.

■ WHY ASK ALL THESE QUESTIONS?

The process that addresses each issue type (see Figure 11.2) is founded on a set of universal questions. They apply to any situation in any industry. The answers change from issue to issue. The questions that gather the relevant information, the formats in which the answers are organized, and the methods for evalu-

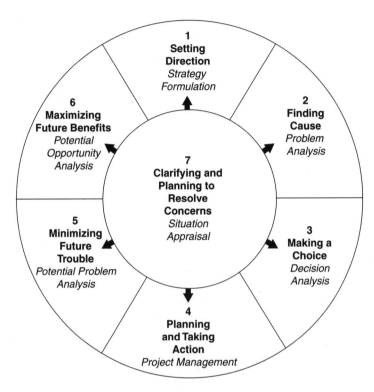

Figure 11.2 The Seven Types of Issues

ating the answers remain the same. They represent a common language for issue resolution that is akin to the patois used by marketers, information technologists, or engineers. Imagine the communication benefits of being able to address an issue via the same terminology and with the same approach. Imagine the effectiveness and efficiency of meetings in which everyone is on the same step at the same time. Imagine the value of having a shorthand through which people can communicate issue information across departments, shifts, time zones, and countries.

■ IS THIS ANYTHING MORE THAN COMMON SENSE?

Good sense? Yes. Common sense? Unfortunately, no. Issue resolution is simply thinking. It is what goes on in individuals' heads as they convert inputs (issues that demand attention) into outputs (solved problems, choices, implemented actions). Each of the seven issue types requires a different thought process. Effective and efficient issue resolution requires mental discipline. Individual discipline pays dividends; organizational discipline pays exponential dividends.

■ WHAT ARE TYPICAL WEAKNESSES IN ISSUE RESOLUTION?

Typical weaknesses in issue resolution are:

- *Failing to adopt a common approach to issue identification and resolution.* For example, in a typical decision-making meeting, one person is pushing a preferred option. Another is pointing out the risks entailed with any option that surfaces. A third is attempting to record benefits. And a fourth is wondering why this group is in the room. Each of these activities has a role in the decision-making process; however, if they go on concurrently, communication is not occurring and progress is not being made.
- *Making a decision before a problem's cause is known.* A doctor may be able to treat your symptoms immediately. However, you will not be cured if the doctor does not understand—or at least have a sound theory about—the disease that is giving rise to your symptoms.
- *Making decisions without appropriately balancing benefits and risks.* Some people focus on the upside and are blind to the risks of a possible course of action. Others' decisions are driven by risk avoidance. While the emphasis on benefits and risks has to fit the nature of the decision and the style of the decision maker, both need to be in the equation.
- *Focusing on problem solving rather than problem avoidance.* In many cultures, problem solvers are elevated to hero status. They have no incentive to avoid problems and, in dysfunctional environments, may even be encouraged to start fires so they can save the day by putting them out. While problem avoidance is rarely sexy, it costs less, takes less time, and inflicts less damage to reputations than allowing a problem to surface.

- *Poorly implementing good decisions.* There are more good strategic and operational decisions that have failed due to poor execution than bad decisions that have taken root. If you fail to take the steps, devote the resources, build the commitment, and exercise the discipline to implement your decisions, your decision making was an academic exercise.

- *Failing to insulate plans against the events that could derail them.* No matter how elegant and comprehensive your plan, it can be impeded—or even halted—by a variety of factors. For example, you could run into unforeseen resistance, conflicting priorities, loss of resources, lack of skills, or a clash with the culture. No time investment yields a greater return than identifying what could go wrong and taking action before it does.

- *Failing to identify and address opportunities.* The volume of problems to be solved and avoided could fill your day thinking only of the negative. However, successful business leaders focus as much or more on the positive. Solving a problem fills in potholes. Avoiding a problem ensures that potholes never appear. Capitalizing on an opportunity creates a new road.

- *Failing to break large issues into their component parts.* Many issues, such as those cited in "Issue Type Seven," are not only too large to be addressed while they are aggregated, they are too global to be owned by anyone below the CEO. Nobody below that level is in a position to address "the quality issue," "the cost issue," or "the innovation issue." Worse is the tendency to throw new issues, unresolved, into these buckets. ("That is just another example of our culture problem.") While synthesizing and identifying themes is healthy, issue resolution can only be done one piece at a time. Each issue in these mountains can be resolved if it is chiseled from the mass.

- *Drawing unsubstantiated conclusions.* The heart of the seven processes is a series of questions, the answers to which establish the platform for issue resolution.

- *Drowning in data.* Too much information can be as paralyzing as too little. The challenge in today's world is to extract from the seemingly boundless mound of information that which can improve the resolution of the issue at hand. The seven sets of questions serve that purpose.

- *Failing to involve the right people in issue resolution.* You need to involve the people who have the information required to solve a problem, make an intelligent decision, and effectively implement an action. There are others whose experience and wisdom should be tapped. There are others who should be involved because their support is critical to implementation. On the other hand, involving too many people can slow down the process, compromise a decision (by appeasing all viewpoints), and waste people's time. The "who" dimension of issue resolution is as important as the "what" and "how."

➤ SELF-ASSESSMENT QUESTIONS

➤ *Do we have a common process for identifying and resolving issues?*

➤ *Do we eliminate problems quickly and permanently?*

➤ *Do we make decisions efficiently?*

➤ *Do we tend to choose the right options?*

➤ *Is the information that we need for problem solving and decision making readily available?*

➤ *Do we develop appropriate plans for implementing our decisions?*

➤ *Do we implement our decisions efficiently and effectively? (Do our projects/initiatives achieve their objectives, on time and on budget?)*

➤ *Do we anticipate and take actions to minimize our exposure to potential problems?*

➤ *Do we identify and take action to maximize the likelihood of and benefits derived from potential opportunities?*

➤ *Do we have a process for clarifying and breaking apart complex issues?*

➤ *Do the right people tend to be involved in issue resolution?*

➤ *Do we have a process for disseminating issue resolutions to those who need them, such as other sites that may have the same issue?*

➤ *Do we have a lessons-learned system that captures issue resolutions and enables people to easily access them?*

■ WHAT IS THE PROCESS FOR DESIGNING AN ISSUE RESOLUTION SYSTEM?

This process is quite different from the one that is provided for each of the other Enterprise Model variables. At the highest level, it has only two steps:

1. *Establish individual issue resolution capability.*
2. *Establish an issue resolution system.*

Step 1 is part of the skill set that should be among an organization's *human capabilities* (see Chapter 8). Step 2 is a key part of an organization's *knowledge management* (see Chapter 9).

To double-click on and illustrate Step 1, an issue resolution system begins with:

- A common language.

  Paula Weichert and her team at BHI, the company introduced at the beginning of this chapter, discovered that they needed a common approach to resolving issues. While it should have been obvious that there were different species of issues that required different thought processes, the team had never identified them. They realized that individuals would always have information that was not known to everyone. They understood, and welcomed the fact, that people had different opinions. However, they concluded that they had been suffering from having different methods for processing the information and opinions. This shortcoming particularly hampered cross-functional meetings. They adopted a set of standard approaches—along the lines of the one outlined above—to different types of issues.

- Skills.

  Once the common approach had been created, BHI trained people at all levels in its use. Executive skill development focused on decision making. Troubleshooters received problem-solving tools. Planners were immersed in project management and problem avoidance methodology.

With the foundation of a common language and skills, an organization can pursue Step 2, an issue resolution system. An issue resolution system has these components:

- *Information capture.* Issue resolution is only as good as the information that feeds it. Routine collection of information on the performance of people, machines, and departments can streamline problem solving and decision making.

  BHI's executives understood that a common approach and skills in its use were not enough. They came to realize that a great deal of the delay and pain they experienced were due to the data treasure hunts that were spawned by the emergence of an issue. They launched a campaign, tied to the goals at all levels, to improve the quality and quantity of information available for issue resolution. They used the questions in their issue resolution processes to begin the routine capture of information that related to customer satisfaction, internal quality, supplier performance, cycle time, cost, productivity, and safety.

- *Templates.* Every organization has recurring issues. Efficiency, and often quality, suffer if they are addressed each time with a clean piece of paper. Templates provide problem-solving and decision-making formats that can be populated with the information that is unique to each type of recurring issue.

  BHI identified its recurring issue resolution arenas as preventive maintenance, shipment scheduling, new product introductions/sunsets, hiring, safety accident investigations, sales performance fluctuations, capital purchases, and marketing program launches. They used their new issue resolution methodologies to develop templates—electronic worksheets tailored to specific applications—in each of these areas. They provided digital and human coaching in the use of the templates.

- *Collaboration vehicles.* The organization establishes mechanisms through which teams of people can jointly contribute to the resolution of an issue. Vehicles include face-to-face meetings, videoconferences, digital chat rooms, and networking software packages.

  The overwhelming majority of BHI's issues required collaboration across departments, shifts, and time zones. As a result, the executives decided to purchase a software package that facilitated issue resolution meetings of distributed individuals and asynchronous contributions to analysis or action.

- *Dissemination processes.* Top management creates a culture that encourages the sharing of issue resolution information that may help another organization. (See the discussion of culture in Chapter 7 and "information as power" in Chapter 9.) As soon as a problem is solved, a decision is made, or an action is taken, the owner of that issue is expected to identify others with a need to know and forward the relevant information to them.

Information dissemination does not have to wait for the issue to be resolved. Any performance information that could later fuel issue resolution (for example, machine downtime, cost of sales, customer satisfaction ratings, employee turnover) should be provided to whomever might be able to use it for problem solving, decision making, and action. (See the treatment of measurement systems in Chapter 6.)

> **For years, BHI had worked hard to minimize internal competition and information hoarding. So the culture supported the sharing of information; however, they did not have much to share or a format in which to share it. The BHI issue resolution design team identified the information that should be shared among people, departments, and sites. They then developed processes for routinely distributing that information, live and via their intranet.**

- *Lessons-learned files.* The cornerstone of an issue resolution system is the creation of a lessons-learned database that includes the thinking and results of problem solving, decision making, and project implementation. The value of this database is a function of (1) the degree to which it is populated with valuable information and (2) individuals' ability to access the database, quickly and easily, through key-word searches.

> **As part of their crusade to establish a corporate memory, the BHI team ensured that their collaboration software package also had a repository in which both live issues and resolved issues could be documented and accessed. They put all employees through a short training program that communicated the what/why/how of the system.**

An organization is only as successful as its issue resolution capability. Companies that are nimble and responsive efficiently and permanently solve problems, consistently make the right choices, and cost-effectively execute decisions.

■ NOTES

1. The Problem Analysis, Decision Analysis, Potential Problem Analysis, Potential Opportunity Analysis, and Situation Appraisal processes presented in this chapter are covered more thoroughly in C. Kepner and B. Tregoe, *The New Rational Manager* (Princeton, NJ: Princeton Research Press, 1997).
2. Kepner-Tregoe, Inc. *Engineering the Performance System*® workshop, 1995.
3. Kepner-Tregoe, Inc. *Project Management Workshop,* 1993.
4. Kepner-Tregoe, Inc. *Managing Involvement*®, 1990.

Chapter

Putting It All Together

Humankind has not woven the web of life.
We are but one thread within it.
Whatever we do to the web, we do to ourselves.
All things are bound together.
All things connect.

— Attributed to Chief Seattle

■ WHY SHOULD ORGANIZATION ISSUES BE TREATED HOLISTICALLY?

Chapter 2 discusses the need to understand the external context in which an organization does business. Chapters 3 through 11 each treat one of the nine internal variables in the Enterprise Model. You may now be hoping that the curtain will be raised, revealing a single diagnostic device that tells you which of the nine levers you need to pull in a given situation. Problem A? You need a *strategy*. Situation B? Clearly, you need to work on your *business processes*. Issue C? It is time for a new *structure*.

Unfortunately, organizations are not that simple. Since a business is an integrated system, you cannot effectively address one variable in isolation. Some analogies from science and mathematics:

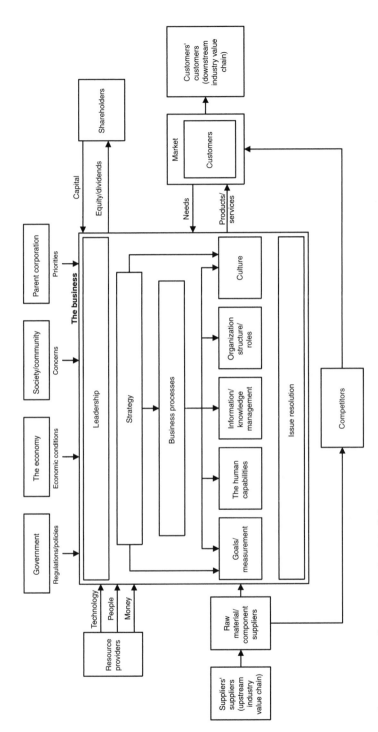

Figure 12.1 The Enterprise Model

213

- You and your doctor cannot treat one organ in the human body without that treatment being influenced by, and having an influence on, others. Organizational organs—the components of the Enterprise Model—are similarly linked.
- You are considering a construction project that would wipe out a species of tiny reptile that, until recently, nobody even knew existed. That seems like a small piece of collateral damage until you understand the role that reptile plays in the food chain in the area. It eats a wide range of insects and, in turn, is part of the diet of two types of rodent. Removing that small link in the chain could have a dramatic impact on the environment in the region. Organizations have similar ecosystems.
- The fluttering of a butterfly's wings in Brazil, through a daisy chain of events, can cause a tidal wave in Japan. In mathematics, this example is frequently used to illustrate chaos theory. In political science, this phenomenon is called "unintended consequences." An organization change can also have effects that are far removed from the point of action.

While all Enterprise Model variables do not need to be treated in all situations, you should recognize that:

> ➤ Any action that you take is likely to influence other variables. A doctor has to be careful not to cure your kidney problem with medication that creates a liver problem. You have to make sure your *information system* medication that cures a knowledge deficit does not create an equally debilitating *culture* problem.

> ➤ The success of any action you take is a function not only of how well you treat the variable on which you are focusing but also how well you address the other variables to which it is linked. Your cholesterol medication will only have its desired effect if it is combined with a dietary regimen and an exercise program. Your *structure* medication will only have its desired effect if it is combined with a treatment of *business processes* and *human capabilities*.

■ HOW DO THE VARIABLES INTERACT?

The need to take an integrated, or holistic, approach to addressing business issues is illustrated by these examples:

- A pharmaceutical company's top executives have considered and rejected acquisition opportunities, new distribution channels, and different pricing models. They have concluded that the best way to meet their ambitious growth targets is through the rapid introduction of successful new products. They can only achieve this *strategy* if:

  ➤ They fully appreciate the needs of potential *customers.* They need to understand needs that customers already perceive (for example, an injection-free treatment for diabetes) and those that customers will perceive only after they have been educated (for example, an inhalant that improves memory).

  ➤ Their *strategy* also defines the boundaries within which all products must fall, describes the markets that the company will serve, and articulates its future competitive advantages. This strategy should be based not only on market intelligence but also on educated assumptions about the future state of *the economy, competition, technology, regulation,* and the *labor supply.*

  ➤ They have an effective, efficient product development *process.* This process includes *suppliers, regulators,* and a wide range of internal departments, including Research and Development, Marketing and Sales, Finance, and Manufacturing. The process should balance the needs for market sensitivity, innovation, compliance, cost control, and speed. It requires a well-oiled subprocess that enables the company to secure patents quickly. The company needs to supplement this product development process with an effective product launch process that includes pricing, promotion, sales, and order fulfillment.

➤ They have a set of *goals* for new product sales. These goals should begin at the top of the house and cascade through the product development and business development processes. Each goal should have a *measurement* system through which accurate actual performance information is regularly captured and provided to those who can use it as the basis for decision making.

➤ Their *culture* supports innovation, speed, and market focus.

➤ They have exemplary *human capabilities* in market research, product research and development, government relations, project management, and business development.

➤ Their *information/knowledge system* supports the product development and launch processes and enables the organization to draw upon the lessons of past efforts.

➤ Their *organization structure* and definition of *roles* support—or at least do not get in the way of—the product development and launch processes.

➤ They have an *issue resolution* tool kit that includes a decision-making methodology that enables them to make go/no-go decisions at the various gates of the product development process, select the new products that will be developed internally and those that will be sourced externally, choose product names, and select the best marketing program. The tool kit should also include techniques for avoiding and removing problems, capitalizing on opportunities, and launching products on time and on budget.

➤ Their *leaders* envision, inspire, enable, and direct all of the above.

Some of these variables are more important than others. However, this company will not be successful if it operates on the assumption that if executives firmly pull one lever—the strategy lever, the business process lever, the goals lever—out will pop the pill that will fuel their growth.

■ Executives at an automobile parts supply company concluded that they could reduce cost and cycle time by streamlining their order-to-cash *process*. However,

➤ Without a link to the business *strategy*, process improvement participants will not understand whether the goal is to establish a competitive advantage, achieve parity, or merely achieve operational efficiencies. If not placed in a strategic context, the process streamlining could actually *remove* a competitive advantage. For example, the company may win based on its customer service, which includes seemingly inefficient customer contact steps throughout the order fulfillment cycle.

➤ If the voice of the *customer* cannot be heard during the process improvement effort, the initiative may fail to achieve its objectives and could even damage relationships. For example, what are the customers' needs in terms of order-to-receipt time? In a just-in-time environment, parts arriving early could be as undesirable as parts arriving late.

➤ If *suppliers* are not wired into the process, it will be suboptimal. The theory of constraints tells us that a process is only as strong as its weakest link. Suppliers—because they are less visible and less within our control—can be that weak link. What specifications, lead times, and payment terms will maintain a seamless partnership?

➤ The improved process cannot be managed on an ongoing basis and continuously improved without *goals*.

➤ The redesigned process may require a change in *culture*. The current reward system may support the highest possible quality but not speed or cost control. The adversarial relationship between sales and manufacturing may encourage minimal contact between those departments. The "just throw the order over the wall" culture clashes with the new process that is based on collaboration throughout.

➤ The process improvement opportunities may lie more in the *human capabilities* than in the sequence of the steps. Perhaps the boxes and arrows in the order-to-cash flowchart make sense. However, plant schedulers lack the skills to sequence multiple complex orders. Outbound logistics personnel do not know the full range of shipping options available to them.

➤ If the process is grafted onto existing *information systems*, it may not reach its full potential. On the other hand, if the process fails to make use of systems that are not going away, it is academic.

➤ If cross-functional interfaces require people to climb the high and slippery walls of the current *organization structure*, the process may fail to achieve its objectives.

➤ The design of the new process is not impervious to problems and is not a substitute for decision making. The company needs an *issue resolution* process that ensures that fulfillment problems are solved and the right decisions are made quickly.

All these variables may not need to change. However, because they have to mesh in a world-class order-to-cash process, all of them need to be considered.

▪ When executives at a consumer products company combined five acquired companies, they recognized that the new *organization structure* would be effective only if:

➤ It reflected the product and market segmentation articulated in their *strategy.*

➤ It facilitated the flow of cross-functional *business processes.*

➤ Its implementation included actions that close *capability, culture,* and *leadership* gaps.

In all situations:

▪ *Strategy* should be based on an understanding of external players such as *customers, suppliers, competitors, investors,* and *regulators.*

- *Goals* should be derived from the needs of the *strategy* and *business processes*. Measurement against those goals benefits from the intelligent use of *information systems*.
- *Human capabilities* and *information systems* should be derived from *business process* requirements.
- *Culture* should support an organization's *strategy* and *business processes*.
- *Issue resolution* tools and systems should fit the work setting established by the *business processes*.
- *Leadership* should fit the *strategy*. (As discussed in Chapter 3, different strategies require different types of leaders.)

There are some single-issue voters. For example, some people base their vote solely on a candidate's position on gun control or offshore drilling or abortion or prescription drug coverage for the elderly. However, a successful candidate cannot take a stand on only one issue. A sports team's competitive advantage may be its scoring prowess, but it does not have the option of playing only offense. A company cannot focus exclusively on quality or cost or innovation. Similarly, managing an enterprise requires monitoring the external environment and the nine internal performance variables. People at all levels should address the needs surfaced by this performance information.

■ DO YOU NEED TO FIGHT A BATTLE ON EVERY FRONT?

The complexity of change initiatives described in these examples could be disheartening. Your reaction may be "I came in for an oil change and the mechanic told me that I need to overhaul the entire engine." Not necessarily. For example, your need for performance improvement may be limited to:

- Closing the *human capability* gaps surfaced in your sales force training needs analysis.
- Installing an *information system* that automates the clumsy, manual steps in your purchasing process.
- Rooting out the risk aversion that represents an unhealthy characteristic of your *culture*.

- Establishing a set of *goals* and a *measurement* system that enables you to track franchisee results.
- Strengthening the *leadership* in your Latin American operation.
- *Resolving an issue*—product damage—that has cropped up in your warehouse.

You do not need to change every variable; you just need to consider the impact of a change on every variable. It is dangerous for you to assume that if you extract one component from an integrated system, fix it or replace it, and install it, everything else will remain the same.

■ WHICH LEVER SHOULD YOU PULL FIRST?

The need should dictate the action that you take first. When confronting deficiencies in some or all of the variables, you probably cannot afford the time and money it would take to address all needs, at least not simultaneously. Furthermore, doing so would probably compromise the ongoing operation of the business. And people have a finite ability to absorb change. The criteria that you should consider when determining which variable(s) to address include:

- Maximize short-term impact on performance.
- Maximize long-term impact on performance.
- Minimize diagnosis/solution design time.
- Minimize diagnosis/solution design cost.
- Minimize solution installation time.
- Minimize solution installation cost.
- Minimize disruption to daily operations.
- Maximize change readiness. (Favor those variables in which people see the need for and are prepared for a different way of doing business.)
- Maximize focus on upstream needs. (Treat those variables that will serve as the foundation for later improvements.)
- Optimize visibility. (You want to be seen as addressing the need. However, you do not want the intervention to be so visible that it blinds the organization to other needs and creates unrealistically lofty expectations.)

The weights on these objectives differ from situation to situation.

So the initial action is based on the situation. However, an "it depends" answer, even if accurate, is never satisfying. Here are some rules of thumb:

- *Address strategic needs before operational needs.* The action plans provided at the end of Chapters Five through Eleven begin with Strategy because it is (1) the bridge between the organization and the outside world and (2) the platform upon which all of the operational variables should be built.
- *Address leadership needs before operational needs.* Should strategy precede leadership or vice versa? This question is fodder for a lively and stimulating barroom debate that will not result in a universal truth; these two variables are tied for first place. An organization with a clear, viable, energizing strategy and visionary, articulate, motivating leadership can compensate (at least temporarily) for weaknesses in the other seven variables. More importantly, that business has laid the foundation for addressing its other needs.
- *Do not wait until you have a performance problem to install a measurement system.* Without goals and a system for tracking and communicating actual performance vis-à-vis those goals, you may not realize that you have deficiencies in one or more of the other variables. Measurement systems are the blood tests that identify viruses before they erupt into serious maladies.
- *Install an issue resolution system as soon as possible.* While issue resolution deficiencies are often less apparent than needs in other areas, problem-solving, decision-making, and action-taking methods are the vehicles through which the other variables' needs are met.
- *Ensure that your business processes are well wired before making changes in human capabilities, information/knowledge systems, and organization structure.* Processes are the way work gets done. If a process is ill directed or ill designed, it will drive development of the wrong skills, information enablers, and reporting relationships.
- *Address culture within the context of a business issue.* There are unquestionably cultural characteristics—trust, collaboration, customer focus, loyalty—that are admirable in all situations.

However, other dimensions of your culture—the degree of openness, the extent of entrepreneurship, the amount of aggressiveness, the priority of cost control—should be based on the unique needs of your strategy and business processes. The trigger for a culture change initiative should be the identification of cultural attributes that are a barrier to achieving the needs of your strategy and/or business processes.

- *Be aware of unintended side effects.* A leadership change may influence strategy. A business process change may influence human capabilities. An information system change may influence culture. Every change should be accompanied by a Potential Problem Analysis and a Potential Opportunity Analysis (see Chapter 11).

➤ SELF-ASSESSMENT QUESTIONS

➤ *Do our leaders take a holistic view of organization improvement needs?*

➤ *Does our strategy guide the identification and resolution of needs?*

➤ *Do we ensure that all improvement efforts are guided by the right leaders?*

➤ *Do we diagnose/troubleshoot our enterprise comprehensively enough to know which variables need to be addressed?*

➤ *Is the scope of our improvement initiatives manageable?*

➤ *Do our improvement efforts deal with the highest priority variables first?*

➤ *Do we consider the impact on other variables before designing a solution?*

➤ *Does our solution implementation treat all of the variables that need to be addressed?*

➤ *Do our organizational improvement efforts build cross-functional, cross-business unit, cross-regional, and cross-process linkages?*

■ WHAT IS THE PATH FORWARD?

There are four ways that you can use the process for addressing each of the Enterprise Model variables:

- *As a comprehensive diagnostic.* In this application, analogous to a complete physical examination, you:

  1. Use the Self-Assessment Questions in each chapter to assess the strength of each of the variables. Every "no" answer is an organizational weakness.
  2. Customize and weigh the criteria in "Which Lever Should You Pull First?" Use them to establish the priority of addressing each weakness.
  3. Take action to address your priority needs, following the process in each chapter that covers a variable you will be addressing.
  4. Use this chapter's guidelines to identify and address the other variables that will influence the success of your intervention.

- *In response to an issue.* You have an issue. Your sales have fallen short of the target. Your profitability growth has stalled. Your cash flow is below expectations. Your stock price is tumbling. You are losing market share, customers, or talented employees. Your quality is declining or your cycle times are excessive. You are lacking role clarity, missing an up-to-date measurement system, or suffering from a cultural deficiency. In this application, you:

  1. Use the guidelines in Chapter 11 to determine the species of issue you are facing (for example, a problem with an unknown cause or a decision).
  2. Follow the process, outlined in Chapter 11, that fits the type of issue you are facing.
  3. As you select or design the action that will resolve your issue, identify the Enterprise Model variables that you will address.

4. Follow the variable treatment processes in the relevant chapters, being alert to influencing variables that may also need to be addressed.

■ *In response to a recommended change.* Someone has recommended a change such as a reorganization, a training program, a culture change initiative, or an information system upgrade. In this application, you:

1. Identify the business need(s) that the change is intended to address.

2. Use this book's Enterprise Model framework, questions, and guidelines to challenge the recommendation. Determine whether the recommendation addresses the appropriate variables (pulls the right levers).

3. Request a cost-benefit analysis, which will enable you to evaluate the merit of the recommendation and assess its priority vis-à-vis other needs.

4. If the recommendation is approved, make sure that the implementation plan addresses all of the variables that will influence success.

■ *As a change management tool.* You are about to initiate a change, or someone else has designed or conceived a change and you will be playing a role in its deployment. In this application, you:

1. Follow the change process that appears in Figure 7.2.

2. Use the Enterprise Model framework and the detailed guidelines for each variable to ensure that the change initiative is pulling the right lever(s) with the right torque.

3. Use the guidelines in this chapter to ensure that the change plan is addressing the variables in the right sequence.

4. During implementation, be alert to the possible need to address unforeseen needs in the variables that will influence success.

Your organization is an organism that is as complex as the human body. As such, you will never completely comprehend every nuance of its behavior and every dimension of its improvement needs. However, the Enterprise Model provides a comprehensive framework that should enable you to understand your organization more fully, identify its highest priority needs, and address those needs in ways that will ensure lasting performance improvement.

Index